ANCIENT-FUTURE
TIME

ANCIENT-FUTURE SERIES

Current Titles

Ancient-Future Faith: Rethinking Evangelicalism for a Postmodern World (1999)
Ancient-Future Evangelism: Making Your Church a Faith-Forming Community (2003)
Ancient-Future Time: Forming Spirituality through the Christian Year (2004)

Forthcoming Titles

Ancient-Future Spirituality
Ancient-Future Communion

ANCIENT-FUTURE
TIME

Forming Spirituality through the Christian Year

ROBERT E. WEBBER

BakerBooks
Grand Rapids, Michigan

© 2004 by Robert E. Webber

Published by Baker Books
a division of Baker Publishing Group
P.O. Box 6287, Grand Rapids, MI 49516-6287
www.bakerbooks.com

Printed in the United States of America

Library of Congress Cataloging-in-Publication Data

Webber, Robert.
    Ancient-future time : forming spirituality through the Christian year / Robert E. Webber.
        p.   cm.—(Ancient-future series)
    Includes bibliographical references and index.
    ISBN 10: 0-8010-9175-6 (pbk.)
    ISBN 978-0-8010-9175-9 (pbk.)
    1. Church year. 2. Spiritual life—Christianity. I. Title. II. Series: Webber, Robert. Ancient-future faith series.
    BV30.W384 2004
    263'.9—dc22
                                            2004011195

To my grandchildren

Tommy Welch
Ben Welch
Jack Welch
Lexi Welch
Quinn Wilson

who fill my life with the joy
of childhood once again.

CONTENTS

TABLES

INTRODUCTION TO THE ANCIENT-FUTURE SERIES

This book, *Ancient-Future Time: Forming Spirituality through the Christian Year*, belongs to the Ancient-Future series. In each book of the series I present an issue related to faith and Christian practice from a particular point of view, namely, that of drawing wisdom from the past and translating these insights into the present and future life of the church, its faith, worship, ministry, and spirituality.

In these books I address current issues in the context of three very significant quests taking place in the church today. First, these books speak to the longing to discover the roots of the faith in the biblical and classical tradition of the church. I affirm the Bible as the final authority in all matters of faith and practice. However, instead of disregarding the developments of faith in the church, I draw on the foundational interpretation of the church fathers and the creeds and practices of the ancient church. These are sources in which Christian truth has been summarized and articulated over against heretical teaching.

Second, this series is committed to the current search for unity in the church. Therefore, I draw from the entire history of the church together with its many manifestations—Orthodox, Catholic, and Protestant— particularly the Reformers and evangelicals like John Wesley and Jonathan Edwards. I weave insights from these traditions into the text so the reader will understand how other deeply committed Christians have sought to think and live the faith in other places and times.

Finally, I use these biblical, ancient roots together with insights and practices from Christian history to constitute the foundation for addressing the third issue faced by today's church: How do you deliver the authentic faith and great wisdom of the past into the new cultural situation of the twenty-first century? The way into the future, I argue, is not an innovative new start for the church; rather, the road to the future runs through the past.

These three matters—roots, connection, and authenticity in a changing world—will help us to maintain continuity with historic Christianity as the church moves forward. I hope what I cull from the past and then translate and adapt into the present will be beneficial to your ministry in the new cultural situation of our time.

ACKNOWLEDGMENTS

No one is fully able to acknowledge all the sources and people who contribute to the writing of a book. Many unnamed books, people, and even institutions have formed my life and challenged me to be sensitive to the work of the church as it moves into a post-Christian world. The fact that I mention only a few of these people and institutions here in no way diminishes my appreciation for the unnamed.

First, I need to thank Northern Seminary for my appointment as the William R. and Geraldyne B. Myers Professor of Ministry. This generous chair has substantially reduced my teaching load, allowing me more time to write. I am equally grateful to Baker Books and especially to Robert Hosack for the support given to this series and for the freedom they have given me to develop this book in a way that reflects my convictions.

Next, there are those special people who have encouraged me and helped me with research and the process of many rewrites and editorial changes. A special word of thanks to Lois Stück and Chad Allen for their careful editing. Thanks to Ashley Gieschen and Barbara Wixon at Northern Seminary for their cheerful and willing help. Finally, and certainly not the least, I owe a debt of gratitude to my wife, Joanne. The freedom she gives me to spend long hours at writing and editing is a gift without which this book would be no more than unfinished thoughts.

INTRODUCTION

I have written *Ancient-Future Time* to introduce the Christian year and the spirituality it orders. As the subtitle declares, the goal of this book is to help individual Christians and local churches learn how their spiritual lives may be formed through the practice of the Christian year. I draw on both Scripture and the ancient Christian practices of the church to show the reader how personal devotion and corporate spiritual worship may be ordered by the Christian year.

We live in a time of great cultural and spiritual transition, a time when many Christians are growing weary of a faith that is shaped by culture and the practices of the world. Many younger evangelicals and older ones as well are searching the past to find ways of spiritual formation that have deeply affected the spiritual lives of many generations. The Christian practice of time is one of the most powerful means of ancient spirituality, and it is currently being rediscovered by the church.

Because the purpose of this book is to encourage individual Christians and congregations to practice Christian-year spirituality, I have not attempted to deal with the historical origins of the Christian year nor have I pursued the developments of the Christian year through the centuries. Readers who want this information will find it from books I have listed in the bibliography.

Let this book serve as a primer. To help the beginner in this ancient discipline, I have included a chart at the end of each chapter. The chart summarizes the main points of each chapter for quick review. Following is a seasonal prayer and then questions for personal or corporate reflection. Finally, some resources on preaching and worship are presented. All these resources are found in the book *Services of the Christian Year* and include Christian-year texts, prayers, confessions, music and the arts, and model services.

Begin your pilgrimage into Christian-year spirituality by reading and reflecting on the chart *Christian-Year Spirituality at a Glance*. This will provide you with a quick overview of the entire discipline. As you delve into each season in future chapters, it will be helpful to have the full year in mind.

I hope you will discover the deep evangelical nature of the Christian year and find spiritual inspiration for your personal life and helpful ancient resources for congregational worship.

Table 1: Christian-Year Spirituality at a Glance

Season	Emphasis	Spiritual Challenge
Advent (coming)	Readiness for the coming of Christ at the end of history and at Bethlehem (the four Sundays before Christmas day).	Repent and be ready for the second coming of Christ. Allow an eager longing for the coming of the Messiah to be birthed in your heart.
Christmas	The fulfillment of Israel's longing. The Messiah has come. The prophecies have been fulfilled. The Savior of the world has arrived (from December 25 through January 5).	Embrace an incarnational spirituality. Let Christ be born within in a new way.
Epiphany (manifestation)	The manifestation of Jesus to all as Savior not only for the Jews but for the whole world (January 6).	Make a new commitment to allow Jesus to be manifest in and through your life.
After Epiphany	A journey with Christ in his ministry as he manifests himself as the Son of God through signs and wonders (the period after January 6 to the beginning of Lent).	Learn to manifest the life of Christ through the witness of life and deeds.
Lent (spring)	A time to travel with Jesus toward his death. Although Jesus is under constant attack, he ministers effectively to the crowds. Lent follows the gathering storm (begins Ash Wednesday, six-and-a-half weeks before Easter; includes Palm Sunday and ends at sunset on Thursday of Holy Week).	Lent is a time for repentance through self-examination and renewal through identification with the journey of Jesus. A time for prayer, fasting, and almsgiving.
The Great Triduum (the three great days)	The most crucial time in the history of salvation. The church recalls in its worship the events of Maundy Thursday and Good Friday. The Great Paschal Vigil of Saturday night concludes with the resurrection Eucharist (the Thursday, Friday, and Saturday of Holy Week).	The three great days are a time for fasting and prayer. We commit to live in the pattern of Jesus' death and resurrection, the pattern of life into which we have been baptized.

Easter (the Christian Pass-over—known as the paschal mystery in the early church)	A celebration of the great saving event of the death and resurrection of Jesus for the salvation of the world. The most crucial event of the Christian year and the source of all Christian-year spirituality (extends for fifty days after Easter, includes Ascension Day, and ends on Pentecost).	Here is the source of the spiritual life. We are called to die to sin in the death of Jesus and to rise to the life of the Spirit in resurrection spirituality.
After Pentecost	The church is born on Pentecost Sunday with the coming of the Holy Spirit. After Pentecost witnesses the spread of the gospel and the growth and trials of the early church (from Pentecost Sunday to the beginning of Advent—about a six-month period).	A time to embrace the teaching of the church and to go deeper into the truths of God's saving events in history.

ORDERING YOUR
SPIRITUAL LIFE

If we can speak so emphatically of the intrinsic value of the liturgical year, it is because we celebrate it together with Christ himself. The special nature of the church year is entirely due to the fact that the Lord himself presides over it and that he celebrates his mysteries with the church for the glory of the Father.

Adrian Nocent

I often talk with my wife about the advertising we see on television. It seems to us that advertising appeals to the "you can get something for nothing" mentality of our culture. Buy this hair product, this juicer, or this car and it will change your life. The product doesn't sell itself as much as the fulfilled life it will bring.

In this way advertising suggests that the good things of life simply fall into one's lap. But experience teaches otherwise. We have to work for what we want. An education, for example, requires years of committed study and discipline. Likewise, character comes from choosing what is right. The virtues of honesty, integrity, and fidelity, for example, require sustained choices of the will. Most of us know that if we are to attain anything that is good, we must do so through disciplined work. What is true about life in general is equally true about spirituality. But what is spirituality?

What Is Spirituality?

Objective Spirituality

At the outset we need to distinguish between objective and subjective spirituality. Objective spirituality, which is our standing before God, is a *given* spirituality. It comes to us as a gift. Because of our sinful condition, we cannot earn or acquire a relationship with God. It is God and God alone who establishes a relationship with us through the work of Jesus Christ. God became man to do for us what we cannot do for ourselves. As incarnate God in Jesus Christ, God paid the penalty for sin, overcame the power of evil, destroyed death, and began the new creation. By his death and resurrection he has rescued us from our alienation to God and restored our relationship with him. This is the gospel preached by Paul, the early church fathers, the Reformers, and the leaders of evangelical awakenings such as St. Francis, John Wesley, and Billy Graham.

This objective spirituality is best described by Paul:

> But God, who is rich in mercy, out of the great love with which he loved us, even when we were dead through our trespasses, made us alive together with Christ (by grace you have been saved), and raised us up with him, and made us sit with him in the heavenly places in Christ Jesus, that in the coming ages he might show the immeasurable riches of his grace in kindness toward us in Christ Jesus. *For by grace you have been saved through faith; and this is not your own doing, it is the gift of God*—not because of works, lest any man should boast. For we are his workmanship, created in Christ Jesus for good works, which God prepared beforehand, that we should walk in them.
>
> Ephesians 2:4–10, italics added

Subjective Spirituality

Subjective spirituality, on the other hand, is a spirituality that arises out of our response to God's grace. The Holy Spirit, whom the Nicene Creed calls the "giver of life," quickens our will to embrace disciplines that express our relation to God. Through these disciplines we *experience* our union with God, a union that God himself has established through the work of Christ and the life-giving power of the Spirit.

The biblical teaching that subjective spirituality is a response to God's grace can scarcely be denied. The apostle Paul made it the central theme of his life when he said, "For to me to live is Christ" (Phil. 1:21). He wanted his life to be conformed to Christ by dying to self and rising to new life in him (Col. 2:12–13). Because Paul saw Christ as the second

Adam, the definitive reality of redeemed human nature (Rom. 5:12–21), he claimed that we who are in him are to be like him. We are to share in his sufferings. We are to become like him in his death. We are to know the power of his resurrection (Phil. 3:10).

The key to the experience of subjective spirituality is expressed by Paul when he adds the word *with* to several compound verbs. I suffer *with* Christ, am crucified *with* Christ, die *with* Christ, am buried *with* Christ, am raised to live *with* Christ, am carried off to heaven and sit at the right hand of the Father *with* Christ (Rom. 6:3–11; 2 Cor. 1:5; 4:14; Gal. 2:19–20; Eph. 2:5–6; Col. 2:20). What Paul is describing here is a profound experience of a relationship with Christ that comes as a result of the choices we make. Tersely put, the message is this: I must "put on Christ" (Gal. 3:27). That is, I am to assimilate Christ; I am to pattern my life in, with, through, and by Christ. I am to experience what Paul experienced when he testified, "I have been crucified with Christ; it is no longer I who live, but Christ who lives in me" (Gal. 2:20). But where do we find the metaphor, the image of our union with Jesus Christ?

Baptism: The Image of Objective and Subjective Spirituality

Both objective and subjective spirituality are brought together by Paul in the image of baptism. In Paul's writings baptism discloses God's grace in which we are united to Jesus and reveals the pattern for Christian living in which we walk in continuous union with him.

We are baptized into the very death and resurrection of Jesus. By his death he overcame death. By his resurrection he makes all things new. Baptismal spirituality is to die to sin and be resurrected to the new life. Paul writes, "We were therefore buried with him through baptism into death in order that, just as Christ was raised from the dead through the glory of the Father, we too may have a new life" (Rom. 6:4 NIV). Think of it! In the simple act of baptism made in faith, we enter into the profundity of the meaning of Christ's death and resurrection. Christ enters into us and we into him. We are now called to live in the pattern of his death and resurrection. And it is Christian-year spirituality that helps us live in our baptism, for it is ultimately an ordering of our lives into the pattern of dying to sin and being raised to the new life in Christ.

The Christian Year as a Pattern of the Spiritual Life

Ancient-Future Time presents the historical understanding of the Christian year as life lived in the pattern of death and resurrection *with* Christ. This spiritual tradition was developed in the early church and has been passed down in history through the worship of the church. It enjoys biblical sanction, historical staying power, and contemporary relevance. Through Christian-year spirituality we are enabled to experience the biblical mandate of conforming to Christ. The Christian year orders our formation with Christ incarnate in his ministry, death, burial, resurrection, and coming again through Advent, Christmas, Epiphany, Lent, Holy Week, Easter, and Pentecost. In Christian-year spirituality we are spiritually formed by recalling and entering into his great saving events.

This book not only describes the Christian year but prescribes how the Christian year can form the spiritual life and shape congregational spirituality. It shows how the practice of the Christian year organizes our internal spiritual experience and brings our everyday experience into union with Christ.

Failed Attempts to Form the Spiritual Life

Before I develop the theme of ordering the spiritual life through the Christian year, I want to reflect on my previous experience of seeking a way to turn my life into a life *with* Christ. My impression is that my own floundering experience is common to most of us. Consequently, I suspect you will be able to identify with some of the examples from my own experience.

As far back as I can remember I was told that Christ should be at the center of my life. As a child I had a plaque on my bedroom wall that proclaimed, "Only one life, 'twill soon be past; only what's done for Christ will last." A day never went by without my seeing these words, without them registering on my life their demanding message and making a lasting impression. This message was reinforced by the church, especially the Sunday-night sings that included songs such as, "Be like Jesus, this my song, In the home and in the throng; Be like Jesus, all day long! I would be like Jesus."[1] I was called into a continuous relationship with Christ, but I was also told that the way to attain spirituality was through the behavior code: "Don't do anything that you would be ashamed to do in front of Jesus, and don't go where you can't take Jesus"—an older version of "What would Jesus do?" Of course these are fine admonitions, and I don't deny their value. But how do you work them out in your life? How can you "be like Jesus"? How is your life a life *with* Christ?

In the fundamentalist tradition in which I grew up, this meant that you didn't go to the movies, smoke, drink, play cards, tell dirty jokes, or hang out with non-Christians. On the positive side it meant that you were to be chaste, honest, obedient, thrifty, and courteous, and you were to work hard at everything. While I now look at this list of *do's* and *don'ts* as rather superficial, I do sense and honor what was at work in these instructions. The truth these admonitions sought to teach was the Christian calling to moral uprightness and to the simple and basic virtue of being a good person. Certainly there can be nothing wrong with that basic message. And when we live by Christian virtue, there is a sense in which we are living with Christ.

As I grew older and attended college and graduate school, my concern to be like Jesus continued to focus on the moral relationship with Jesus, but it grew to include an intellectual pattern of spirituality. For me, being with Jesus became learning to think out of a Christian worldview.

Truths about the origin, meaning, and destiny of life were to inform my worldview and make me a Christian in my mind, in the pattern of my thoughts, and then in my lifestyle. I embraced Jesus as the ultimate source of meaning in life, the one through whom existence was defined. He became the integrating core of my studies, the center for faith and learning, the beginning and end of knowledge. Today I continue to appreciate this emphasis. I confess that Jesus Christ is the cosmic center of the universe, the one in whom all things consist (Col. 1:17–20), the one through whom meaning is derived.

But I still looked for more, much more. What I longed for was something that went deeper than pious ideas on morality or intellectually stimulating thoughts about the meaning of human existence, as good as these were. I wanted something that actualized the pattern of being in Christ. I wanted something that worked in my life, something that brought a realistic spirituality into being. I wanted something that ordered my life into the pattern of Christ's life, death, resurrection, and coming again.

In the early '70s I came upon an ancient discipline for ordering the Christian life. It is the spiritual discipline of living in the pattern of Jesus' saving life throughout the year. This discipline is so filled with depth and so challenging to the spirit that I feel I have, after a number of years, only begun to scratch the surface of its potential. It has the power to call ethical behavior into conformity with the pattern left us by Jesus. It has the power to construct a view of reality that is thoroughly Christian. But more, it compels us to live, die, and be raised with Christ. Through the discipline of the Christian year we can experience the power of Christ within the community of the church, through its worship and in our lives twenty-four hours a day, seven days a week.

Now the question is: How can the discipline of the Christian year do this? How can the Christian year order our entire lives—our values, worldview, and personal relationships; our struggles with lying, cheating, lust, jealousy, anger, and such; our ambitions and drive for success, material wealth, power, and recognition; our complicity with the hunger, injustice, and pain of the world? How can the discipline of the Christian year lift us up into Christ so that the cry of Paul, "For to me to live is Christ" (Phil. 1:21), is fulfilled in greater measure within us? I want to answer that question by looking first at the nature of the Christian year and then showing how the church and its worship is the context for ordering the discipline of a Christian-year spirituality.

At this point you may be saying, "You're attaching too much significance to the Christian year. It is impossible for the discipline of the Christian year to accomplish so much for my spirituality." This objection has validity if the Christian year is seen as an end in itself. However, if we see the Christian year as an instrument through which we may be shaped by God's saving events in Christ, then it is not the Christian year that accomplishes our spiritual pilgrimage but Christ himself who is the very content and meaning of the Christian year.

Christ: The Source of Christian-Year Spirituality

As we think of our spirituality shaped through the practice of Christian time, it is of utmost importance that we begin with Christ, who is the source of our spirituality and the one who gives meaning to time. Without Christ there could be no Christian time. It is Christ who determines the Christian year, and it is through the practice of Christian-year spirituality that Christ is formed within us.

By *Christ* I mean the mystery of Christ born, living, dying, and being raised again for the salvation and healing of both creature and creation. Therefore, what gives rise to the Christian year is the *paschal mystery* (the oldest term used for Easter). The church is called to proclaim continually and act out this central mystery of God's reconciling work in Jesus Christ as it journeys through time from year to year, month to month, day to day, and hour to hour. For this reason the Christian year has been defined by Adolf Adam as "the commemorative celebration, throughout a calendar year, of the saving deeds God accomplished in Jesus Christ."[2]

The saving deeds that God accomplished in Christ are historical events. They are not mythical ideas or powerful stories but true, real, concrete events through which the God of creation acted within history to rescue the fallen world. The very heart, center, and focal point of all God's saving activity is the passion and resurrection of Christ. Consequently, the very heartbeat of time, the source of meaning and power for the cycle of all time, *derives from* and *returns to* the death and resurrection of Christ in which God was uniquely active reconciling us to himself (2 Cor. 5:18). It is Christ in his saving event who is the source, the summit, and the very substance of both objective and subjective spirituality.

This principle, that one *primordial* event shapes spirituality, reaches back into the Jewish tradition as well. Even though Jewish spirituality is marked by a number of events commemorating God's action on behalf of Israel (Feast of Weeks, Feast of Succoth, Rosh Hashanah, Yom Kippur, Hanukkah, and Purim), it is above all else the Passover feast that is central for Jewish spirituality. This feast remembers Israel's deliverance from Egypt. In this exodus event God acted decisively to liberate Israel from the clutches of the enemy, to bring them out of their oppression, to constitute them as his people, and to lead them into the Promised Land.

Moses was told that when the children asked about the meaning of Jewish spirituality, the story of the exodus was to be told. "Then you shall say to your son, 'We were Pharaoh's slaves in Egypt; and the LORD brought us out of Egypt with a mighty hand; and the LORD showed signs and wonders, great and grievous, against Egypt and against Pharaoh and all his household, before our eyes'" (Deut. 6:21–22). The source, the summit, the very substance of Jewish spirituality is grounded in the exodus event.

Consequently, the later development of the Passover seder as a way of recalling God's redemption for Israel was more than a desire to tell the story again. What is behind the Passover seder is a concern to *experience* the redemption, to enter into a relationship with the Redeemer, and to serve the Redeemer by keeping his commandments. So the story is relived not simply for the sake of the story but for the purpose of living an exodus spirituality.

The relationship between Jewish and Christian spirituality is obvious. It is no accident that Christ was crucified during the Passover season. Consequently, the early Christians quickly saw the relationship between the redemption of Israel and the new redemption in Christ. Paul spoke of "Christ, our Passover lamb" (1 Cor. 5:7 NIV). Here we have the earliest record of the Easter celebration. But this early Christian feast was no mere recollection of a historical event as an end in itself. Like the Jewish Passover seder, *it recalled an event to transform life.*

The Christian Passover is a passage from the clutches of the evil one. The evil one would have us, as an ancient baptismal catechesis warns us, to live by the works of the flesh—"fornication, impurity, licentiousness, idolatry, sorcery, enmity, strife, jealousy, anger, selfishness, dissension, party spirit, envy, drunkenness, carousing and the like" (Gal. 5:19–21). The Christian Passover celebrates that to which we have been transformed. So the same ancient baptismal catechesis describes our new life as: "the fruit of the Spirit is love, joy, peace, patience, kindness, goodness, faithfulness, gentleness, self-control" (Gal. 5:22–23). This transformation is a transition from allegiance to the evil one to an allegiance to Christ.

Paul puts it this way: "Those who belong to Christ Jesus have crucified the flesh with its passions and desires" (Gal. 5:24).

Christian-year spirituality is nothing less than the calling to *enter* by faith into the incarnation, the life and ministry, the death and resurrection of Jesus. God's saving action is not only presented to us through the practice of the Christian year, it also takes up residence within us and transforms us by the saving and healing presence of Christ in our lives. As we enter the saving events of Jesus and especially the paschal mystery in faith, Christ shapes us by the pattern of his own living and dying so that our living and dying in this world is a living and dying in him.

I have found this spirituality to be an endless source of challenge, a rhythm for spiritual awakening, and a pattern for a daily dying to the power of evil and rising to the power of Christ. But we are not asked to do this spiritual calling alone. It is a calling for me, for you, and for all God's people that is accomplished in the context of a community—the church.

The Church: The Context for Christian-Year Spirituality

As we attempt to understand how our spirituality may be ordered by the discipline of the Christian year, we must keep in mind that the death and resurrection, which is the source and foundation of the Christian year, is not an event that is frozen in a particular historical moment. True, it is an event that happened at a particular time and place in history. But because it is an event of eternal significance, it transcends the particulars of time and space and relates to all of time—it reaches back to the purpose of creation and forward to the end of history. Now the question is: Where is this Christian discipline of the Christian year practiced? The answer: in the church.

Although there are many different ways to speak of the church, one of the most significant images of the church in the New Testament is "the people of God" (see Rom. 9:25–26). We, the people of the church who have been born into Christ, are the sons and daughters of God in whom the Holy Spirit dwells. We are the people of the Christ event. The church now lives on earth between the historic saving event of the death and resurrection and the future coming of Christ when the transformation of the world will be completed. The church has been entrusted with the meaning of all time. The world does not know the meaning of its own history, but the church does. Through the discipline of the Christian year, the church proclaims the meaning of time and of the history of the world.

Peter spoke directly to how the church witnesses to the meaning of time when he reminded the Christians of the dispersion, "You are a chosen race, a royal priesthood, a holy nation, God's own people, *that you may declare the wonderful deeds of him who called you out of darkness into his marvelous light"* (1 Peter 2:9, italics added). The purpose of the church is to be a sign of the redemption as it declares the wonderful *deeds* of God in Christ accomplished in history and fulfilled at the end of time.

The very nature of the church is defined by the saving deeds of God in Christ. The church, as the extension of Jesus in the world, is called to be an incarnational embodiment of Jesus' *way of being*. It is not just another institution in the world (although it allows itself to degenerate into that on occasion), but it is the *sign* of the historic redemption and of the coming kingdom. The church witnesses to God's saving deeds not only by its very existence in the world but also by its worship, which animates its life.

Worship Expresses Christian-Year Spirituality

How does the church express the spirituality of being *with* Christ in his incarnation, manifestation to the world, death, resurrection, ascension, and coming again? How can we as members of the church participate in a present spirituality that is rooted in past events and anticipates a future event? The answer to this question is that we are shaped and formed spiritually by Christ in the church through a worship that continually orders the pattern of our spirituality into a *remembrance* of God's saving deeds and the *anticipation* of the rule of God over all creation.

In order to help us understand how the church and its worship forms our spirituality through memory and anticipation, I will first define worship and then relate that definition to the practice of Sunday worship and of the Christian year.

Worship Defined

In its most simple and basic sense, worship is a celebration of God's mighty deeds of salvation culminating in the death and resurrection of Christ. Worship celebrates historic events that happened in the past and anticipates the eschatological event that will happen in the future. It does so in such a way that the meaning of both past and future is made alive in the believer's experiences now. Through worship the worshiper enters into God's saving deeds through which the entire history of the world is revealed.

Unfortunately, many churches have lost contact with this biblical and historical tradition of worship and have turned it into an invention of their own making. Some see worship as a school. Sunday morning is primarily a time for teaching. What happens before the sermon is regarded as preliminaries or warm-up for the sermon. Recently I spoke to a very frustrated pastor from this tradition who now has a biblical understanding of worship and really wants to lead his people in worship. He said, "But what they want is a song, a prayer, and a fifty-minute teaching." He went on to say, "When I try to introduce the Christian year, they think I'm going liberal. They come to me and say, 'Drop all that stuff, pastor, and just get to the Word.' They don't seem to grasp that the Christian year is the Word proclaimed and enacted."

There are other ways contemporary churches fail to celebrate God's saving deeds as the central focus of worship. In some churches, as one pastor said, "We celebrate our own experience with Christ." Other churches have turned toward a psychiatric approach to worship, using worship as a time to help people discover themselves and their potential in life. Others lean toward entertainment or turn worship into an opportunity for evangelism.

You may respond, "If these are not appropriately biblical forms of worship, what is?" That is a fair question and one that must be answered if we are going to understand how a worship that follows the Christian year can shape our spiritual lives.

What does it mean to say, as I have stated above, that worship *celebrates God's saving deeds culminating in Christ*? To understand this statement, keep three things in mind. First, consider what God has done through Christ by the power of the Holy Spirit. Christ has redeemed the world by his death and resurrection. Through Christ the power of evil has been overcome. Paul states, "[God] disarmed the principalities and powers and made a public example of them, triumphing over them in him" (Col. 2:15). In doing so, "In Christ God was reconciling the world to himself" (2 Cor. 5:19). Consequently, we know that both creature and creation "will be set free from [their] bondage to decay and obtain the glorious liberty of the children of God" (Rom. 8:21). This is the gospel. The message is that God has reclaimed his world and won it back from the clutches of the evil one. Jesus is the victor over sin, death, and hell. He is the second Adam. "For as in Adam all die, so also in Christ shall all be made alive" (1 Cor. 15:22). "Therefore, if any one is in Christ, he is a new creation; the old has passed away, behold, the new has come" (2 Cor. 5:17). So God is pleased with the work accomplished by the Son. There is nothing in this world that gives God greater pleasure—not the angels, not creation, not our faith in him, not our service. God's greatest pleasure is in his Son, who has accomplished the redemption of the world.

Second, what brings glory to God is to celebrate what gives God the greatest pleasure. Because God is most pleased with the work of his

Son, he loves to have us celebrate the mighty deeds of redemption. For this reason worship arises from the paschal (Easter) mystery. As author Robert Taft has written, "True worship pleasing to the Father is none other than the saving life, death and resurrection of Christ."[3] In worship, then, we tell and act out God's saving deeds, culminating in the living, dying, rising, and coming again of Christ.

Third, we tell and act out God's saving deeds so that the power God exhibited through Christ in overcoming evil and reclaiming creation may take hold within our lives. The purpose of worship is not only to glorify God by celebrating the work of his Son but also to assimilate in our own lives the pattern of dying to the sin that Christ died to destroy and rising to the new life that Christ rose from the dead to inaugurate. Because worship celebrates Christ, worship calls us to put off the "old man" and put on the new. Worship calls us to "put to death therefore what is earthly in you: fornication, impurity, passion, evil desire, and covetousness" (Col. 3:5). Worship calls us to "put on then, as God's chosen ones, holy and beloved, compassion, kindness, lowliness, meekness, and patience" (Col. 3:12; see also vv. 13–17). Worship recalls the Good News; it awakens faith within us; it stimulates us to die to sin and rise to the new way of life in Christ Jesus. In this way worship relates to all of life and extends into every relationship, every task, every attitude, every action, every day, and every hour of our lives. In this way we fulfill the admonition of Paul: "I appeal to you therefore, brethren, by the mercies of God, to present your bodies as a living sacrifice, holy and acceptable to God, which is your *spiritual worship*. Do not be conformed to this world but be transformed by the renewal of your mind, that you may prove what is the will of God, what is good and acceptable and perfect" (Rom. 12:1–2, italics added).

To summarize, the impact of a worship that remembers God's saving deeds and anticipates God's ultimate reign over all creation orders our spiritual experience of being *with* Christ. The thankful recalling of God's saving deeds and the joyful anticipation of the new heavens and the new earth is the heart of weekly Sunday worship and the very substance of the pattern of Christian-year worship. Let me explain.

Sunday Worship: The Day to Remember and Anticipate

The early church set aside the day we now call Sunday as the day for the weekly recall of the living, dying, and rising of Christ and the day to anticipate the future kingdom. Robert Taft sums up the importance of Sunday for the early Christians and gives us an insight into the spiritual depth Sunday recalls.

29

To anyone beginning the study of Sunday in early Christian literature, the initial impression is one of confusion: Sunday is the first day, the day of creation, the day of light, the day of a new time. But it is also the last day, the eighth day, the day beyond days, the day of Jubilee, the day of the end-time. It is the day of resurrection, but also the day of the post-resurrection appearances and meals. It is the day of the descent of the Spirit, day of the ascension, day of the assembly, day of the Eucharist, day of baptism, day of ordinations—until one asks, "is there *anything* Sunday *doesn't* mean?" The answer, of course, is no. It was *the* symbolic day, sign of the time of the church between ascension and parousia, the time in which we are living now. It is the day symbolic of all days, for the purpose of all Christian liturgy is to express in a ritual moment that which should be the basic stance of every moment of our lives.[4]

The importance of Sunday as the day of God's saving deeds may be seen by noting the names given to Sunday by the early church. Probably the oldest name given to the day is "the Lord's day" found in Revelation 1:10. "The Lord's day" may have originated from the phrase "the Lord's Supper," which was celebrated every Sunday in the early church as the central act of worship (see 1 Cor. 11:20).[5] The Lord's day is his day because it is the day the church gathers to celebrate his death, resurrection, and anticipated return through the breaking of bread, the Lord's Supper, the communion, or the Eucharist.

Another term that captures the meaning of Sunday is the *eighth day*, a term frequently used by the early church fathers. The *eighth day* refers to the new day of the re-creation. God made the world in six days, rested on the Sabbath, and then on the first day of the week (Sunday), the day of the resurrection, began his work of re-creation. Thus the eighth day is the day of the recapitulation, the day that God makes all things new through Christ.

More recently the original meaning of Sunday as the day of God's saving deeds is being restored due to liturgical scholarship. This rediscovered meaning of Sunday is captured in the document on the Sacred Liturgy from Vatican II:

The Church celebrates the paschal mystery every seventh day, which is appropriately called the Lord's Day or Sunday. For on this day Christ's faithful are bound to come together into one place. They should listen to the word of God and take part in the Eucharist, thus calling to mind the passion, resurrection, and glory of the Lord Jesus. . . . The Lord's Day is the original feast day, and it should be proposed to the faithful and taught to them so that it may become in fact a day of joy and of freedom from work. . . . Sunday . . . is the foundation and kernel of the whole liturgical year.[6]

The Christian Year: Unfolding the Whole Mystery of Christ

Everything said above about Christ as the source of spirituality, the church as the center of spirituality, and worship as the expression of spirituality pertains in an unequivocal way to the Christian year.

> In the course of the year, moreover, she [the church] unfolds the whole mystery of Christ from the incarnation and nativity to the ascension, to Pentecost and the expectation of the blessed hope of the coming of the Lord.
>
> Thus recalling the mysteries of the redemption, she opens up to the faithful the riches of her Lord's powers and merits, so that these are in some way made present for all time; the faithful lay hold of them and are filled with saving grace.[7]

The simple, unadorned purpose of the Christian year is to proclaim the gospel of God's saving deeds *with* Christ, especially in his death and resurrection.

The Christian year represents the historical unfolding of the life of Christ and his sure return. One may observe that Advent deals with the coming of Christ; Christmas, his birth; Epiphany, his manifestation to the Gentiles; Lent, his journey toward death; the Great Triduum, the last days of Jesus' earthly life; Easter, the time to celebrate his resurrection; and Pentecost, the time to experience life in the power of the Holy Spirit. According to this historical representation of the life of Christ, the Christian year begins with Advent and ends with Pentecost. Indeed, the practice of most Christians who follow the Christian year is to follow the chronological sense. Piety is then based on this pilgrimage throughout the year. That this historical representation of God's saving events has been of spiritual benefit to God's people cannot be denied.

However, when the Christian year is turned into a mere repetition of the past, we miss the point. The spiritual purpose of celebrating God's saving events is to be formed by Christ, to die with him, to be raised with him, to be born anew, and to live in the hope of his resurrection and return.

Again, let me take Christian-year spirituality back to its roots in Jewish spirituality. Adrian Nocent observed, "For the Jew, God is involved in history, but for God, the past, present and future coexist. . . . The Jewish liturgy is envisaged as an act that allows a being whose existence is transitory to come into contact with him who always is; he who always is comes into contact with him whose existence is transitory."[8]

For the Jew to commemorate the past is not merely to recall it as a past event but to commemorate it in such a way that it gives the present new meaning. Therefore the Jew is called upon to commemorate the Passover as though it is happening *now*. At the same time the commemoration of the past event has a future reference. The Passover, for example, looks forward to the day when all will gather in Jerusalem. Consequently, the past and the future converge on the present in *such a way that it makes a difference in the worshipers' experience now*.

This formative approach to God's saving events is shared by the early church fathers. For example, writing of the effect of the work of Christ celebrated in the Christian year, St. Leo stated: "Beloved, the remembrance of what the Savior did for mankind is most useful to us, provided that what we venerate in faith we also receive and imitate. For in the communication of the mysteries of Christ to us, there is present both the power of grace and the encouragement which teaching gives, so that we may follow by our deeds him whom we confess in the spirit of faith."[9]

Conclusion

Now we must ask: What does all of the above mean for those of us who wish to practice Christian-year spirituality? First and foremost, Christian-year spirituality drives us back to the death and resurrection of Jesus Christ. The source of spirituality does not lie in us. We cannot generate, create, or attain spirituality. Jesus Christ, who is God incarnate, became one of us to pay the penalty for sin, to overcome the powers of evil and death, to rescue us from the evil one, and to restore our relationship to God. Everything that ever needed to be done to make us acceptable to God has been done by Jesus.

Second, to embrace Christian-year spirituality means that we must once again embrace the biblical image of baptism. Baptism is our identification with Jesus Christ. It is the metaphor of our union with his death and resurrection. Baptism calls us to die to sin and to be raised to the new life in the Spirit.

Third, Christian-year spirituality calls upon us to acknowledge that this new identity, this baptismal life, is not lived in isolation but in community. While we live our baptismal life in the world, the church is the context in which the baptismal life is nurtured. The baptismal life is birthed in the womb of mother church, nourished at her breasts, and animated by her spirit.

Fourth, to live a Christian spirituality the worship of the church must return to its biblical roots in the paschal mystery. While every Sunday is a remembrance of the death and resurrection and an anticipation of the end of history and the transfigured world, Christian-year spirituality is ordered by the succession of Sundays that enter into the mystery of the incarnation, ministry, death and resurrection, and coming again of our Lord.

As we enter into the very life of Christ, his life interpenetrates our lives, and we learn to live in the pattern of his life and death as we die to sin and rise to new life in Christ. In succeeding chapters this theme will be developed in detail to show us how to be shaped by Christian-year spirituality personally and corporately.

Table 2: A Summary of Christian-Year Spirituality

Theme	Spiritual Emphasis
What is objective spirituality?	A relationship with God cannot be earned. It is the gift of God's grace.
What is subjective spirituality?	The disciplines of spirituality intensify our experience of living *with* and *in* Christ.
What is Christian-year spirituality?	A discipline of personal and corporate worship through which we are formed into Christlikeness. We intentionally enter into Christ by living in the pattern of his saving deeds and anticipating his rule over all creation.
What is the *source* of Christian-year spirituality?	The source is the death and resurrection of Jesus Christ.
What is the *context* of Christian-year spirituality?	The context is the church.
What is the church?	The people of God's saving events who by their very existence witness to God's saving deeds.
How is Christian-year spirituality expressed?	It is expressed in worship.
What is worship?	The remembrance of God's saving deeds through proclamation and enactment and the eager anticipation for God's rule over all creation.
What is Christian-year worship?	The unfolding of the mystery of salvation.
What is the purpose of Christian-year spirituality?	To become so thoroughly identified with God's saving events that we live in the pattern of dying to sin and rising to new life in Christ.

A PRAYER FOR CHRISTIAN-YEAR SPIRITUALITY

Almighty God, unto whom all hearts are open, all desires known, and from whom no secrets are hid: cleanse the thoughts of my heart by the inspiration of your Holy Spirit, that I may perfectly love you and worthily magnify your holy name by the practice of Christian-year spirituality; through Jesus Christ my Lord. Amen.

Adapted from *The Book of Common Prayer*

Questions for Reflection

1. Describe how you currently practice time.
2. What steps do you need to take to practice a Christian-year spirituality?
3. What steps need to take place in your local church to incorporate the Christian practice of time?
4. What difference would it make in your personal spiritual life to practice Christian-year spirituality? What difference would it make in the life of your church?

Resources for Worship and Spirituality

At the end of each chapter I will cite the resources for each season contained in Robert Webber, ed., *The Services of the Christian Year*, vol. 5 of *The Complete Library of Christian Worship* (Peabody, MA: Hendrickson, 1994). This is a fairly exhaustive resource for all seasons of the Christian year. Available through www.ancientfutureworship.com or 630/510-8905.

ONE

THE CYCLE
OF LIGHT

The primary focus of worship and spirituality during the cycle of light is the incarnation of God into our history to rescue creatures and creation. He was born to die that we might live.

The meaning of the incarnation does not stand alone. The connection between birth and death is confessed in the Nicene Creed (AD 325). The one who became incarnate is "God from God, Light from Light, True God from True God." The reason he became incarnate is "for us and our salvation he came down from heaven . . . for our sake he was crucified under Pontius Pilate."

Isaiah, the prophet of Christ's coming, puts it well: "Surely God is my salvation; I will trust and not be afraid. The LORD, the LORD, is my strength and my song; he has become my salvation" (Isa. 12:2 NIV).

While the incarnation is the central focus of the cycle of light, our worship and spirituality is characterized by three experiences that give fullness to the incarnation—Advent, Christmas, and Epiphany. Each of these periods of spiritual journey relate to the incarnation in their own special way.

During Advent we *wait*. In this time we recall Israel's longing for the Messiah, and we learn to yearn for the second coming—the eschatological end of history as we know it and the beginning of the new heavens and new earth.

During the days of Christmas we *rejoice*. The Messiah has come. The light of the world has been born. A new day has fallen upon us.

During Epiphany we *manifest*. We now know that this momentous new beginning is not only for the Jews but for

all the peoples of the world and for the whole of creation. God has come. The promise of old that the world will be rescued from the tyranny of evil has now been made real.

We wait (chapter 2).

The Christ child has come (chapter 3).

The world must be told (chapter 4).

ADVENT

A Time When God Breaks In on Us

The first coming of Christ the Lord, God's son and our God, was in obscurity;
the second will be in the sight of the whole world. When he came in obscurity
no one recognized him but his own servants; when he comes openly he
will be known by both good people and bad. When he came in obscurity,
it was to be judged; when he comes openly it will be to judge.

Augustine (AD 354–430)

For many of us late summer and early fall is a time to make new plans
for the coming year, the year that is organized around the academic calendar. For example, my own personal time is occupied with the making
of syllabi, meeting new students, and planning a year's curriculum and
events. Families with children spend a great deal of time getting ready
for school—buying new clothes and school supplies. Once school starts
the pressure is on with old and new friends, the demands of classes, and
participation in sports and other activities.

For those of us who live in the colder climates, fall is also a time to
prepare for winter. We gather wood for the fireplace, rake the leaves,
seal the storm windows, winterize the car, get winter clothing out of
storage, and prepare ourselves to dig in for the winter months.

But where is God in all of this? The danger we all face as we prepare
for the future, whether it is for our fall activities or something else, is
the tendency to be indifferent to the presence of God in our plans. We

participate in that humanistic spirit prevalent in our Western world, a spirit that often expresses itself in the way we plan for the future. When we think we can do things on our own, we act as though we have little or no need of God. Then we become self-confident, begin to believe in ourselves, and think ourselves to be invincible.

When this happens God becomes remote and even absent from our lives. We may go for days without any sense of God, without recourse to prayer, or without concern to hear God speak to us through his Word. At the same time the religious practices in which we engage—prayers before meals and attendance at Sunday worship—take on a ritualistic and somewhat meaningless character. We do them as one might run a machine in a mindless job, and they mean little to us. They have no power, and God does not reach us through them. They have become dead forms, lifeless and without meaning.

To say we did not mean for this to happen would be an understatement. None of us wants God to become remote and removed from our lives. Nevertheless God sometimes becomes distant. Perhaps we cannot trace back to the point at which we became spiritually indifferent. But we know the aliveness to God we once had has dissipated and is now lost in our personal experience. Perhaps we have not chosen to let God be in our lives. We live quite comfortably with God at a distance.

In times like these our personal experience is akin to Israel's before the birth of Christ. It is also similar to the condition of the world today, a world that is still largely indifferent to its Creator, the one who alone can give it meaning and purpose. Our lives as well as those of Israel, the church, and the world pass through rhythms of cold indifference, and then God breaks into our lives and we become open and receptive. In the twists and turns of these alterations we are called to a new awareness of life, to new commitments, to a new conversion of the soul. Whenever this happens an Advent has occurred, for Advent is the time when God breaks in on us with new surprises and touches us with a renewing and restoring power. In Christian-year worship and spirituality we call upon God for a new breaking in, a fresh outpouring of his Spirit.

Advent: A Time When God Disturbs the Waters of Our Lives

Not far from my home there is a stagnant pool of water. Although the children of the area find it to be a great pond for ice skating in the winter, it is otherwise useless except as a place for scampering bugs and croaking frogs. So far as I can tell, the water is absolutely silent. Nothing runs into it. Nothing runs through it. Nothing runs from it.

Unfortunately our spiritual lives sometimes become like this stagnant pool of water—dead, barren, still, and unproductive. In the time of Isaiah, one of the central figures in Advent, Israel had grown stagnant. Israel was not unlike the pool of water near my home, undisturbed by any flow into it or out of it. But through Isaiah God began to stir up the waters to renew Israel and bring the hope of new life. During Advent we turn to Isaiah to hear how God can stir up the waters of our dead spirituality and refresh us with a new spring of clear and lively water of life.

Who is this man Isaiah? What was his world like? What did he have to say to the people of Israel? If we can answer these questions we will see why Isaiah is the prophet above all prophets chosen for the Advent season. The Israelites had become indifferent to God and God's claim over their lives. So Isaiah's calling was to prepare the people so that God could break through their indifference and become real to them again. The message Isaiah delivered to Israel revived them and, even more, transcended their time and pointed to the coming of the Messiah. Today Isaiah's message transcends our time and points not only to the Messiah's birth in Bethlehem but to the coming again of the Messiah, to the age of peace and God's reign over the whole world. As the message of Isaiah turned the hearts of Israel toward spiritual renewal, so that message today in Advent or in any time when we need a fresh coming of God in our lives can stir up the waters of our stagnant spirituality and cause God to break in on us in a fresh way.

Isaiah's Advent Hope

One of the most important credentials Isaiah brought to his prophetic ministry in Israel and his continuing influence in our lives today was that he was a man who lived in the presence of God: "In the year King Uzziah died I saw the Lord sitting upon a throne, high and lifted up." And he heard the seraphim singing, "Holy, holy, holy is the LORD of hosts; the whole earth is full of his glory" (Isa. 6:1, 3).

In Advent worship we are lifted up to sing with the angels, the archangels, and the seraphim, "Holy, holy, holy is the Lord God Almighty, who was and is and is to come!" (Rev. 4:8). Unfortunately, we frequently fail to see what Isaiah saw. We allow the goals, ambitions, and everyday responsibilities of life to be so central to our thoughts that we fail to shut down and center on the Holy One, the Creator, the one who is high and lifted up above all that is. Isaiah saw above the details of his own life and the issues of his nation. By faith he went to the very heart of human existence itself. Like Isaiah we need to get beyond the form of our worship. We need to experience the presence of the one who stands over us to judge us, heal us, and restore us to life.

Isaiah not only saw the Lord, he saw himself for what he was in the presence of the Lord. He cried, "Woe is me! For I am lost; for I am a man of unclean lips, and I dwell in the midst of a people of unclean lips; for my eyes have seen the King, the LORD of hosts!" (Isa. 6:5). In the presence of God, Isaiah saw himself as a sinner in need of God's forgiveness and restoration. Today in worship we are to stand in the presence of the Holy One of Israel and see ourselves as the sinners we really are.

There is also a third aspect of this revelation of God. Even as Isaiah saw his sin, God turned to him in forgiving and restoring love. Isaiah tells that a seraphim flew to him, touched his lips with a burning coal taken from the altar and said, "Behold, this has touched your lips; your guilt is taken away, and your sin forgiven" (Isa. 6:7). When we meet God and confess our sin, God forgives us and restores us. Here is the rhythm of the gathering in worship—the procession brings us into the very presence of God. We praise God in his transcendence, we confess our guilt, and then we hear the words of forgiveness. Then, and only then, are we ready to hear God speak to us in the service of the Word.

This rhythm in Isaiah's experience is not only a compelling picture of Isaiah's preparation to speak God's word to Israel but also a moving account of the experience with God that is available to us in every worship and then is presented to us in a new and intense way in the experience of Advent. Isaiah's experience illustrates the rhythm of Advent: If we would see God, if God is to break in on us, we must see ourselves for what we are. Then, in our moment of honest self-recognition, God will break in upon us and stir up the waters of our spiritual lives. This was Isaiah's message to his own people, Israel. This is Isaiah's message to the church today as it lives in Advent waiting.

Isaiah's Political World

Isaiah's world, like our world today, was one of political unrest. The great united kingdom of David, which had been handed over to Solomon, had been split into the northern and southern kingdoms. These two kingdoms were weakened by internal dissension and wars against each other. Then the powerful Assyrian hordes swept down on the northern kingdom, defeating and utterly destroying it in 732 BC. Next, in swift succession Babylon rose to power, defeated the Assyrians, and swept Jerusalem and the southern kingdom into defeat and exile in 587 BC. Soon Babylon was defeated by the power of Persia.

In the middle of these tumultuous experiences Israel was carried away into captivity. In captivity Israel longed for a return of God to favor her, to bring her back to Jerusalem, and to return her to the glory experienced under David. In this context Isaiah spoke out as the conscience of Israel, and in keeping with his own experience he called Israel to repent and turn to God in faithfulness.

Scholars identify three phases of Isaiah's ministry. Because these eras seem so different in emphasis and time, many scholars assume there were three Isaiahs. These critical questions cannot be addressed here, nor do they need to be. Therefore we will treat the three phases of the ministry of Isaiah as a united whole.

In the first part of the book (chapters 1–39) Isaiah set forth what was essential to his message: God wanted the people of Israel to work together with God to shape history. However, the people of Israel were carried off into exile and felt deserted by God. The second part of the book consists of chapters 40–55. Here the message is that God has the power to save Israel and bring them back to Jerusalem. These chapters speak of God's servant who will bring the deliverance. They contain many of the Advent readings that Christians believe refer to the first coming of Christ (see Isa. 52:13–53:12). Finally, the third portion of Isaiah is contained in chapters 56–66. These passages speak of the glorious resurrection and restoration of Jerusalem. Christians see in these passages a direct teaching regarding the second coming of Christ and the restoration of the whole world (see Isa. 65:17–25).

It is against the backdrop of these three phases of Isaiah's ministry that we need to understand the message of Isaiah to Israel and his message to us. We wait for the coming of Christ to rid the world of evil and to establish the new heavens and new earth. In Advent we wait for the new beginning. And in our own lives Advent represents a new beginning, a turning away from sin, and a conversion to Christ.

Isaiah's Advent Message

While Isaiah's message must be understood against the backdrop of the political turmoil described above, it must also be interpreted in the context of the major religious problem in Israel, a problem that cut to the very heart of its spiritual life—dead worship. The worship of Israel, once the source for renewing life, had degenerated into dead ritualism. Isaiah described this condition rather succinctly: "What to me is the multitude of your sacrifices? says the LORD; I have had enough of burnt offerings of rams and the fat of fed beasts; I do not delight in the blood of bulls, or of lambs, or of he-goats" (Isa. 1:11).

It should not be surprising that the worship of Israel had gone sour. The life of worship is not in the ritual itself but in the lives of the people shaped by the message of worship. The spiritual impact of worship is to produce a people who live lives of compassion and justice. Just as God acted justly for Israel and brought her up out of the harsh and unjust treatment of Egypt, so true worship works within God's people the meaning it represents. How far Israel's heart was from God was demonstrated by her lack of justice for the poor and oppressed. Again Isaiah spoke quite directly about Israel's condition of injustice: "Wash yourselves; make yourselves clean; remove the evil of your doings from before my [God's] eyes; cease to do evil, learn to do good; seek justice, correct oppression; defend the fatherless, plead for the widow" (Isa. 1:16–17).

Isaiah was not pitting worship against justice. He was asking for the restoration of worship that results in justice and compassion for the poor. In Israel this divorce between worship and justice resulted in a religious stagnation. The people felt God was absent from them, that he didn't care to break through their lethargy with the waters of new life. But the problem was theirs; they were blocking the flow of God's spiritual renewal by the twin sins of a dead ritualism and a failure to act with justice.

It is in the context of Israel's dead spirituality that Isaiah's message takes on a very real and significant meaning. What is Israel to do? They are to plead with God to break through their stagnant and insensitive attitude and to shake them of their lethargy. They are not to be content with what they have. They are to be dissatisfied with the status quo, to loathe the mere keeping of worship as a religious duty.

Consequently at the center of Isaiah's message is the cry to repent. But for Isaiah repentance is not a mere matter of the will. Israel cannot simply decide to repent and be done with it. No, repentance comes from God. God must bother Israel. God must interfere with the lives of the Israelites, break into their pattern of selfish behavior, smash their pious self-centeredness, and turn them away from the hardness of their hearts. Isaiah pleaded with God: "Oh LORD, why dost thou make us err from thy ways and harden our heart, so that we fear thee not? Return for the sake of thy servants, the tribes of thy heritage" (Isa. 63:17).

It is this state of repentance, this condition of readiness that God wants for Israel. For when the people of Israel turned from their sins and prepared themselves for a breakthrough from God, God was able to come to them with a new experience that would turn their lives upside down and change the history of the world. Isaiah promised a breakthrough from God in two prophecies: "Therefore the Lord himself will give you a sign. Behold, a young woman shall conceive and bear a son, and shall call his name Immanuel" (Isa. 7:14). "For behold, I create new heavens and a new earth; and the former things shall not be remembered or come into mind. But be glad and rejoice for ever in that which I create; for behold, I create Jerusalem a rejoicing, and her people a joy" (Isa. 65:17–18).

To summarize, Isaiah offers Israel hope. If they will repent and turn from their sin, God will send them a Savior who will lead them out of their exile and return them to a rebuilt Jerusalem, a new city that will be greater than they can even imagine.

The Application of Isaiah's Message to Advent

If we are to enter into Advent in a truly spiritual and meaningful way, we must keep in mind the messages of Isaiah to Israel. The people of Israel were in a deplorable circumstance. Their lives, homes, nation, families, wealth, and positions in society were threatened by an impending political disaster that would throw them all into ruin. In addition they were in no spiritual condition to go through such a catastrophe. Repent, turn to God in true conversion, proclaimed Isaiah. Then hope in God's rescue, for God will surely send you a Savior and restore the greatness of Jerusalem.

How does this apply to us today in the Advent season? Advent is always needed when we, the people of God, separate our lives in the world from the true meaning of worship. Worship celebrates God *for us* and works within us the desire to be servants to others and to the world. When we go about our lives striving for power, success, and wealth and seek *things* for ourselves and yet attend worship, listen to the Word, and take bread and wine into our stomachs, we are no better than dead Israel. God cannot be in our worship because God is not in our lives. Our worship becomes mechanical, dull, dreary, and rote. Our lives drift further and further away from God and from his will, and the sense of God's absence becomes more and more acute. That is what happened to Israel.

Advent is a time when we ask, even plead with God not to leave us alone, for when God leaves us to our own choices and turns us over to our own ways, we are certain to drift from him. Our indifference to God is soon turned into spiritual boredom, a boredom that leads to spiritual inertia and ultimate death to spiritual realities. Advent is a time to cry, "O God, turn me away from my indifference, create in me a heart of repentance, and lead me to the waters of spiritual refreshment." The Advent sequence known as the *Rorate Caeli* sums up this heartfelt cry:

We have gone astray;
in the multitude of our sins we have been made unclean.
Fallen, fallen, stricken as the leaves of autumn.
The storm wind carries us away,
the tempest of our evil deeds.
You have turned us from the face of your mercy,
and our iniquity has crushed us like a potter's vessel.

O Lord our God, look upon your people in their affliction; be mindful
of your promises.
Send us the Lamb who will set up his dominion from the rock of the
wilderness to Zion, enthroned on her mountain.
There is no other whose power can break our chains and set us free.[1]

Advent is not only about our repentance and conversion, it is also
about the expectation of the Messiah who will come to deliver us.
During Advent we look for the coming of the Messiah in Bethlehem
(Micah 5:2–4) and the coming of the Messiah at the end of history
(Isa. 65:17–25; Rev. 20–22). For Christians both of these Advents are
rooted in the paschal mystery. The cross is the goal of the Messiah's
coming. Incarnation and atonement are inseparably linked as are
the atonement and the second coming because he came to redeem
and rescue creatures and creation. He came to reclaim the creation,
to wrest it away from the clutches of evil, to rid it of the presence
and power of evil, and to ultimately restore it to a new heavens and
a new earth.

In Advent we celebrate the beginning and ending of Christ's victory
over the powers of evil, and we call upon God to accomplish that
victory in our own lives, to break in on us, to be born in our hearts,
and to create us anew. This is the message of Isaiah to us: a Savior is
coming not only to Israel but to the whole world. This is the message
that becomes intensified by John the Baptist and Mary, who encounter
us with the dramatic call to an expectation of the Christ child who will
accomplish the eschatological redemption of all things.

Advent: A Time to Live in the Expectation That God Will Break Through

Jewish people know what it means to live in hope. The misfortunes
of Isaiah's day and succeeding troubles of the Jewish nation have
produced within them a vital sense of the future. For Jews it is always
"next year, in Jerusalem."

Just before the birth of Christ we find this throbbing hope alive
in an Israel in bondage to Rome. The longing for the messiah to
come and deliver Israel is alive in many groups of truly sensitive and
spiritually alive people. Two such people who figure largely in our
Advent hope are John the Baptist and Mary. Both of them teach us
what it means to live in expectation of a dramatic deliverance from
the power of the evil one.

John the Baptist: An Advent Voice

In the days of John the Baptist an expectation for the coming of the messiah was running high. In every Jewish circle the discussion of a soon-coming messiah was at a fevered pitch. There was a sense that the eschatological moment of a new beginning for Israel was just around the corner. But how would the dreams of Israel come true? Would God inaugurate this new exodus through a new Messiah?

In this context of dreams, hopes, and aspirations, John the Baptist appeared out in the desert to call people to repentance and preparation for the coming age. Picking up on themes from Isaiah he startled the Jewish community with his message, "Repent, for the kingdom of heaven is at hand" (Matt. 3:2).

It was significant that John the Baptist came from the desert and was born in an unusual way. The people of Israel were aware that God's prophets emerged from the desert, that they were born under unusual circumstances, or that they were characterized by an unusual sign of their special appointment. For example, David, a mere boy with no experience in battle, defeated Goliath; Moses was found in a basket and saved from death. Now here was John the Baptist, born of a woman who had been barren for years but now in her old age gave birth to a prophet under unusual circumstances, a prophet who had emerged from the desert.

So when John the Baptist came on the scene in such a dramatic way, the attention of Israel was immediately directed to him. Was he the Messiah? Was he the one who would lead Israel out of its bondage to Rome and restore Jerusalem to greatness? What Israel wanted was a political Messiah, a redeemer like Moses and David combined.

But John the Baptist had a clear vision of himself. He saw himself as the precursor, the forerunner, the one who was to prepare the way for the Messiah as foretold by Isaiah (Isa. 40:1–11). He called Israel to a true repentance fitting the occasion of a new exodus. And he pointed to the one who was to come saying, "I baptize you with water for repentance, but he who is coming after me is mightier than I, whose sandals I am not worthy to carry; he will baptize you with the Holy Spirit and with fire" (Matt. 3:11). St. John described John the Baptist as "a man sent from God. . . . He came for testimony, to bear witness to the light, that all might believe through him. He was not the light, but came to bear witness to the light" (John 1:6–8). And bear witness to the light he did, for John the Baptist was the one who pointed to Jesus and said, "Behold, the Lamb of God, who takes away the sin of the world!" (John 1:29). The Jews were looking for a political Messiah—a new Moses or a new David. But John, by designating Christ as the Lamb of God, spoke of the vision of the servant Yahweh whom Isaiah had described in chapter 53 of his prophecy. John the Baptist saw Jesus as the Passover lamb, the new spiritual redeemer.

One evidence that John the Baptist is an Advent voice to us is that he confronts us with the message that God uses people in our lives to tell us the truth about ourselves. He was by his very lifestyle as well as his words a confrontation, calling people to repentance and conversion of life. We need to ask whether there is a John the Baptist in our lives who, unpleasant as it may be, points out by his or her example a sinful habit or desire in our lives with which we need to deal. Perhaps God cannot break through to us until we have dealt with our sin decisively. Repentance is not the favorite pastime of Christians; we would rather hide our sinful desires, habits, and attitudes than give them over to God. We put off repentance as we hide behind our good works, attendance at worship, or involvement in the life of the church. Perhaps this is the time to deal with that relationship, that falsehood, the spirit of anger or jealousy, that attitude of racism or sexism, or that complicity in injustice. Let that modern John the Baptist whom God has placed in your life be a stimulus to repentance and conversion.

Next, John the Baptist is an example of the kind of person God can break in upon and use. He was a person whose sole mission in life was to serve God. He wanted nothing for himself. He shunned fame, wealth, and family to do God's bidding. He had no thought for self and gave all he had to point to Christ and not to himself. We hear the reading of his ignoble death at the cunning request of Herodias's daughter (Matt. 14:1–12), but we fail so often to truly understand John the Baptist and feel his pain. His life, his convictions, his priorities, and his death call us to take a serious look at ourselves. What kind of vessel are we for God's use? Do our ambitions and dreams tie into the aspirations of worldly success so that God cannot break through to us and use us to touch others with Christ's love and hope?

Third, John the Baptist gave us a clue to our Advent preparation when he answered the question posed to him by the multitudes: "What then shall we do?" His answer was simple and straightforward, "He who has two coats, let him share with him who has none; and he who has food, let him do likewise" (Luke 3:10–11). His answer is a call to self-giving love. Perhaps before God can really break in on us we need to identify someone in need and give to that person or group in a sacrificial way. How can we expect God to pour out a spiritual blessing on us when we are stingy with our abundance? Clinging to our earthly goods only arrests the flow of God's love through us and back to us again. Perhaps the intensity of God's presence in our lives this Advent season will match the intensity with which we are willing to love a creature of God who is less fortunate than we.

Finally, John the Baptist represents the relationship we must have with Jesus. His goal in life was to point to Jesus and Jesus alone. His heart's cry was, "He must increase, but I must decrease" (John 3:30). We must ask ourselves why we do what we do in life. Do we perform works of mercy and charity so people will point to us and remark on our love and generosity? Or do we, like the great figure of Advent, do what we do in order to promote faith and trust in Jesus alone as the second Adam, the Paschal Lamb who brings redemption to the world through the sacrificial self-giving of his life?

If we are to live in the expectancy of God breaking through to us to touch us with saving and healing power, we will do well to look not only to John the Baptist for guidance but also to Mary, the mother of Jesus.

Mary: An Advent Voice

Isaiah, John the Baptist, and Mary all have one thing in common—they lived in expectancy of the coming Messiah. But of these three Advent personages, Mary's relationship to Jesus is of a special nature because it was in her womb that the Messiah was conceived, it was in her womb that the Messiah grew, and it was from her womb that the Messiah was born. For this reason it is appropriate for us to burst forth in praise to Mary's role in redemption and say with Elizabeth, "Blessed are you among women, and blessed is the fruit of your womb!" (Luke 1:42).

We know very little about Mary, about her person, her life, her family. Nevertheless, what we do know is that her role in bringing the Messiah into the world reveals a person of substantial character and spiritual commitment. She was "a virgin betrothed to a man whose name was Joseph," a woman who had "found favor with God," a woman who was to "bear a son, and . . . call his name Jesus" (Luke 1:26–31).

From these few facts we can discern first that Mary was a woman in whom the hope of Israel was alive. Even though the expectancy of a messiah was running high and was a much talked about hope in the circle of Mary's life, it would have been easy for her to ignore this hope or be indifferent to it. After all, as an engaged woman she had much to think about and many plans to make for her future life. But Mary was a deeply religious woman who had not forsaken the longings for a new day for Israel.

Next, we see in Mary a woman who was willing to take a risk. Here she was, a virgin engaged to Joseph when the angel appeared to her and said, "Behold, you will conceive in your womb and bear a son" (Luke 1:31). We have no record of the conversation between Mary and the angel Gabriel except for the angel's announcement and Mary's words, "Behold, I am the handmaid of the Lord; let it be to me according to your word" (Luke 1:38). She didn't say, "But what of my reputation?" or, "Choose someone else, I have other plans." No, she yielded to God's will without a battle, without resistance, without qualifications. Her commitment to the hope of Israel was so deep that she was willing to set aside, if need be, her own plans and ambitions in order to fulfill the will of God for her life.

In addition to these qualities Mary also had a profound understanding of the Messiah's mission. The song of Mary, know as the *Magnificat* (Luke 1:46–56), expresses the hope of Israel as it is drawn from the prayer of various psalms. Mary knew that the promise made to Abraham was being fulfilled in her; she knew that God was now active in Israel to do a new work for Israel. She also knew that God was on the side of the poor, the oppressed, and the downtrodden, and she knew that redemption was at hand. The revolution that was begun in Jesus was the revolution that would put down the power of evil and eventually do away with evil in the whole world, bringing the world into a new creation—the new heavens and new earth. And Mary, a young virgin thought to be about thirteen years of age, not only understood what was happening but was a direct participant in the dawning of a new beginning. She gave to the Messiah, the Redeemer of the world, the human person in whom God would accomplish the reconciliation of all things to himself.

Indeed, Mary was a remarkable woman, a woman that Advent sets forth as the kind of person we may strive to become. So it is important for us to ask, "What does Mary teach us about our own Advent discipline?" Mary teaches us that when we hope for a visit from God, a new breaking in on us, we ought to be prepared to do what God asks us to do. God may ask us, as he asked Mary, to take a risk. When God breaks through, he often disturbs the complacency of our lives. Perhaps God will ask you to do something that will be misunderstood by your friends and opposed by your family. Perhaps God will ask you to help someone whom most people ignore or to give of your time or money to a needy family, organization, or cause. How will you react? Will you say, "God, I'll do anything but that," or like Mary can you say, "Let it be to me according to your word." Mary's submission to God, her willingness to do God's will without question, is a necessary posture for us if we truly want God to break in on our lives and touch us with the power of a new spiritual awakening.

Mary also speaks to us about our Advent meditation. In the introduction to this book I pointed out how the spiritual discipline of following the church year is more than a mere reconstruction of Jesus' life. I argued that every phase of the church year is rooted in the paschal mystery—the dying and rising to life of Jesus Christ and the promise that in Christ we are born anew even as the world itself will be made new in the end of time (2 Cor. 5:17). Mary moves us to meditate on this redemption because she herself participated in the redemption in such a significant way. Without Mary there would have been no redemption, for without the incarnation there can be no atonement. God became one of us in order to restore us to his image and make us new. This necessitated the role of woman in redemption, for only through the womb of a woman could God receive the flesh and blood of his own creation. This does not put Mary in the position of being a co-redeemer; God reconciled the world through Christ, not through Mary. But Mary's role was indispensable for redemption, and our attitude toward her ought to be as she herself sang: "Behold, henceforth all generations will call me blessed" (Luke 1:48).

The early church fathers reflected seriously on Mary's place in redemption. Without in any way detracting from the work of Jesus Christ to redeem the world, they included Mary in the place the Scripture gives her. Irenaeus, a writer and theologian of the second century, writes of Mary in the following tribute:

> So the Lord now manifestly came to his own, and born by his own created order which he himself bears, he by his obedience on the tree renewed and reversed what was done by disobedience in connection with a tree; and [the power of] that seduction by which the virgin Eve, already betrothed to a man, had been wickedly seduced was broken when the angel in truth brought good tidings to the virgin Mary, who already [by her betrothal] belonged to a man. For as Eve was seduced by the word of an angel to flee from God, having rebelled against his Word, so Mary by the word of an angel received the glad tidings that she would bear God by obeying his word. The former was seduced to disobey God [and so fell], but the latter was persuaded to obey God, so that the virgin Mary might become the advocate of the virgin Eve. As the human race was subjected to death through [the act of] a virgin, so it was saved by a virgin, and thus the disobedience of the virgin was precisely balanced by the obedience of another. Then, indeed, the sin of the first-formed man was amended by the chastisement of the first-begotten, the wisdom of the serpent was conquered by the simplicity of the dove, and the chains were broken by which we were in bondage to death.[2]

Our Spiritual Pilgrimage during Advent

Over the past centuries the liturgy of the church has developed a spirituality particularly for Christians during Advent. Both the Sunday liturgies and the daily Scripture readings have been designed to direct our journey into the Advent experience of the mystery of Christ. Our parents in the faith have chosen Scriptures that accent three Advents: the Advent of Christ coming into our own lives, the Advent of Christ's physical birth in Bethlehem, and the Advent of his second coming at the end of history. While the liturgies and daily readings of Advent begin with the second coming and move as in a funnel toward the first coming, we are called to a vital personal encounter with Christ through all the readings. As we prepare to be enriched by the Advent liturgies and our personal daily readings, it will be helpful for us to think about how we should journey through the season.

Meditating on the Second Coming

The spirituality of Advent calls us to start our journey in expectation of the second coming of Christ. The end time is the period in history when the work of Christ will be consummated, when the powers of evil will be put away forever, when the earth will be restored to the golden age described by Isaiah and St. John (see Isa. 65; Rev. 20–22). How is this hope for a future restoration of the world to guide our meditation?

First, the hope of a world restored under God proclaims that evil is not the final word. If we were to read only the newspaper accounts of murder, espionage, violence, wars, and the like, we would have only a negative view of the world. If we were to visit the hospitals with the terminally ill, the psychiatric wards with the mentally deranged, or the prisons filled with lawbreakers, we would see the world only from this view. If we were to spend all our time among the poor, among those who are starving to death, among those who are oppressed under political or economic systems that dehumanize and depersonalize people, we would have a pessimistic view of the world.

What the second coming says to us is that the evil of this world is doomed. It will be judged and burned by fire because God in Christ has already dealt a decisive blow to the powers of evil. God has dethroned these powers and taken away their ability to have ultimate control over history and over our lives (Col. 2:15).

Next, the second coming says that the ultimate word in history is the triumph of God, the reign of God's kingdom, the eternal and lasting rule of the good. Here is where our Advent meditation rests. By faith we are promised that evil will be judged and done away with and all will be made whole. This is the vision we want to carry with us as we view the news and visit the hospitals, psychiatric wards, and prisons of our world. Christian hope is an optimism about life that is grounded in Christ and celebrated again and again in the liturgy of the church.

Not only do the readings of Advent build this hope up within us, but the eucharistic prayer of the church reminds us: "Father, you loved the world so much that in the fullness of time you sent your only son to be our Savior. Incarnate by the Holy Spirit, born of the Virgin Mary, he lived as one of us, yet without sin. To the poor he proclaimed the good news of salvation; to prisoners, freedom; to the sorrowful, joy. To fulfill your purpose he gave himself up to death; and rising from the grave, destroyed death, and made the whole creation new."[3] Here in this prayer is the hope by which we live, a hope to shape our attitude about life, a hope that determines our relationships to the events of the world, a hope that gets us through the bitter times of sickness, disappointments, shattered dreams, and the fear of death.

Meditating on the Longing for Christ

Advent spirituality is not a time to meditate on the actual birth of Christ. According to tradition, we ought not to sing Christmas carols until Christmas itself, for Advent is not a time to celebrate the birth of Jesus in the manger but a time to long for the coming of the Savior. The appropriate sense of this season is captured in the pleading of "O come, O come, Emmanuel, and ransom captive Israel."[4]

Because Advent is a time of longing for redemption, we should use the Advent season as a period to identify the matters from which we need to be redeemed. Identify whatever it is that seems to be holding you in its power. Take a piece of paper and write at the top, "Powers that hold me in their grip." Then begin to list everything that you can think of from which you would like to be set free. These powers may be bad habits, undesirable relationships, a job that is stifling and unrewarding, a vice such as a bad temper, jealousy, envy, or dishonesty, or any blockage to living by the spirit of joy, temperance, or generosity. Whatever it may be, commit it to the one who comes to set the prisoners free, turn it over to Christ in prayer, and ask the one who is to come into your life to take this problem up into himself.

There is one more matter that is important in this discipline, however. If you would truly turn this issue over to Christ, the decision must come from the inside—from the heart and the will. You must purpose it. One of our greatest problems is that we make our decisions intellectually without recourse to the deeper side of our personality. Obviously the mind must be engaged in our decisions, but decisions of life that are primarily formed in the mind without the pain of a gut-wrenching longing that results in sleepless nights and moments of deep anxiety are too often dismissed with the wave of the hand or a rationalization that seems intelligent and acceptable. In your prayer, plead and petition the God who is coming in Christ to touch you on the inside and to birth in you an anxious and heavy longing to be redeemed from the power that holds you in its grip. Then and only then will Christ come to be born in your heart.

Meditating on the Advent of Christ in Our Lives

In Advent spirituality we are also called on to meditate on the birthing of Christ in our hearts. In this matter we are dealing with the conversion of life, the movement away from the old life lived under the power of evil to the new life lived in the power of the Holy Spirit. True conversion is a turning from one way of life to another. Christ calls us to be converted to him, to make him the pattern of our lives, to make our living and dying a living and dying in him. This can only be accomplished as we completely submit to him and live our lives in respect to his paschal mystery and by the example he left for us to follow.

Advent is a time to review once again where our faith is placed and how our lives are lived. Trust in Jesus is not merely a onetime act but a continuous state of being, a moment-by-moment existence in Christ. It is a daily turning from a life lived for self to a life lived in tune with the power of the Spirit who continually calls us to be like Jesus.

Some people who have lived particularly wild lives find the contrast between their old way of life and their new way of life to be dramatic and vivid. This was certainly the experience of St. Paul, whose dramatic conversion resulted in an about-face. But for many the transfer of allegiance to Christ and to the way of life he calls us to emulate is quieter and less discernible. Many of us who have been reared in Christian homes and nurtured in the faith are not able to point with certainty to the precise moment of conversion. Whether we come into the faith through a stormy and cataclysmic experience or were parented into Christ is not the real issue. What is at stake during Advent is an assessment of our current state of faith and living and our commitment to keep on living in the hope to which we have been called.

Conclusion

Advent asks us to deal with the basics of our relationship to God through Jesus Christ. Do I really believe in Christ? Have I put my hope and trust in him? Do I see the future through the eyes of the one who came to redeem the world from the power of evil? Is there a longing within me for him to be formed within, to take up residence in my personal life, in my home, and in my vocation? These are not easy questions to answer. They require meditation, intention, and above all, a commitment that remains steadfast. But if we would break away from a spiritual life growing cold and a Christ who is becoming distant, we must be attentive to our spiritual discipline and long for God to break in on us with new life. When we do this, we experience the true meaning of Advent spirituality.

Table 3: A Summary of Advent Spirituality

Theme	Spiritual Emphasis
What is the meaning of Advent?	Objectively: Israel's longing for a messiah. Subjectively: A longing for a new breaking in of God's Spirit upon us.
Why is Isaiah the prophet of all prophets for the season of Advent?	Isaiah's message prepared Israel for the coming of the Messiah (first birth) and for his eschatological reign at the end of history.
What kind of spirituality does Isaiah model for us?	He centered on God's holiness; he saw himself as a sinner; God broke in upon him. This is the rhythm of Advent.
What is the *general* message of Isaiah to Israel and to us?	Work with God to shape history. God has the power to save Israel (and us). God will restore Israel (and the world).
What is the *specific* message of Isaiah to Israel and to us?	Your worship is dead! Repent and turn to God. God will send a Savior.
How does the message of Isaiah apply to Advent worship and spirituality?	Plead with God to break in on us. Live in expectation for the coming of God into our lives and into history.
How does John the Baptist image Advent spirituality?	His sole mission in life was to point to Jesus as the coming Messiah. His lifestyle was one of self-giving love.
How does Mary, the mother of Jesus, image Advent spirituality?	She was ready to do what God asked her to do. Following Mary's example, we are to be open receptacles for God. Our prayer comes from her words "May it be to me" (Luke 1:38).
What are the three Advents—the three comings that form our Advent spirituality?	The longing for Christ to come anew into our own lives. His coming at Bethlehem to be our Savior. The expectation that at the end of history he will rescue the world and establish his rule in the new heavens and earth.

A Prayer for Advent

Merciful God, who sent your messengers, the prophets, to preach repentance and prepare the way for our salvation: Give us grace to heed their warnings and forsake our sins, that we may greet with joy the coming of Jesus Christ our Redeemer, who lives and reigns with you and the Holy Spirit, one God, now and forever. Amen.

From *The Book of Common Prayer*

Questions for Reflection

1. How does our moment in history and the state of the church compare to Isaiah's moment in time and to the spiritual lethargy of Israel?
2. How is the message of Isaiah applicable to us today?
3. Which of the three figures of Advent (Isaiah, John the Baptist, or Mary, the mother of Jesus) describes your Advent calling? How?
4. How do you need God to break in on you?

Resources for Advent Worship

The following worship and preaching resources are found in Robert Webber, ed., *The Services of the Christian Year*, vol. 5 of *The Complete Library of Christian Worship* (Peabody, MA: Hendrickson, 1994), 107–53.

- Preaching texts for Advent
- Lighting the Advent candle
- The "O" antiphons
- Traditional opening prayers for Advent
- Prayers for Advent worship
- Advent canticles
- An Advent affirmation of faith
- An Advent eucharistic prayer
- Advent blessings
- The arts in Advent worship
- Sample Advent services

CHRISTMAS

A Time When Christ Is Birthed Within

Christ became the son of man so that we could become children of God.
Had he not so lowered himself as to come down to us, none of us could
ever have gone to him by any merits of our own.

Leo the Great (AD 400–461)

Most of us can dig deep into our memories and find a Christmas or two
from way back in our childhood. Two of my earliest childhood memories
of Christmas provide a stark contrast to each other.

I grew up in the jungles of the Belgian Congo (now the Republic of
Congo). One of my most distinct memories of Christmas is a celebration
in Mitulu, my parents' mission station, deep in the beautiful forest land
of Africa, one hundred and fifty miles away from the nearest town. Our
compound sat in an open area surrounded on three sides by the jungle
and on the remaining side by a small, bold, protruding mountain where
one could find cannibal remains. Here and there from the craggy rocks
were wild bushes and flowers and through them, winding lazily up the
mountain, was a well-worn path taken by pilgrims who for centuries
climbed to the top of that mountain to look at the vast and beautiful
space of the African forest.

Christmas was a very special day in the lives of these African
Christians—not because they exchanged gifts or decorated trees, but
because on this day they had a unique way of celebrating the incarnation.

Early in the morning the people of the village gathered at the foot of the mountain, hiked up the winding pathway, gathered the colorful wild flowers, and then slowly proceeded down the mountain singing Christmas carols. This ceremony was culminated as they stood around our mud home, planted their flowers around the mission quarters, and sang more songs of the birth of God's Son. I love to recall the mystery, the joy, and the peace of it all.

My second memory goes back to my first celebration of Christmas in Ventnor, New Jersey, at the Houses of Fellowship, a group of furlough homes for missionaries. I was seven. On Christmas morning we got up to a room full of Christmas presents under a tree. I had never seen such an array of gifts, and I couldn't wait to dive into those presents. But first, my father told us, we had to read the Christmas story and pray. I didn't hear a word except the "Amen," and then I dove into the presents like someone who had never received a gift.

As I look back on those two experiences, the first one in Africa impressed me with the mystery of it all. We were celebrating something that we couldn't entirely understand. But the African Christians, true to their more primitive relationship to the mystery of nature, chose a poetic and symbolic gesture as the way to celebrate Christmas meaningfully. That experience has stuck with me all these years, and I have yet to exhaust its meaning.

The second experience in America did not impress me at the time with anything other than the sense of the overwhelming abundance and my good fortune in receiving more gifts than I knew what to do with. However, as I now reflect on that experience, I am drawn to the contrast between the reading of the Christmas story and the abundance of gifts: something heavenly and divine and something earthly and human juxtaposed. In an uncanny way this second memory speaks to me of the incarnation of God in Christ—the divine presence in human form.

These two images—mystery and incarnation—are at the heart of our spiritual pilgrimage during Christmas. Let me elaborate on both.

Experiencing the Christmas Mystery

I know of no better way to get into the meaning of the mystery that happens at Christmas than to walk through the major Christmas festival, the ancient vigil of Christmas Eve. I have not always attended this vigil, so the memory of my first Christmas Eve vigil service is still vivid in my mind. In a moment I'll reflect on that service, but first I want to comment on my old way of celebrating Christmas.

I'm embarrassed to say that my experience of Christmas before becoming more mindful of the ancient way of celebrating Christmas is less spiritually stimulating than I prefer to remember. In my church there was always a special candlelight service of singing along with a children's pageant. But this always occurred on the Sunday night before Christmas, and since we had no Advent preparation, it simply appeared in the middle of my normal routine of life, which differed little from that of the secular world. Nor did Christmas ever carry any special spiritual meaning. When I was single and when I was married without children, it was a night for a good, clean, fun party. As soon as the children came along it was the night to get them down and kept down so Santa could arrive with the toys. Christmas day was like my experience in Ventnor—a reading of the story, opening of presents, a delicious dinner, and time with family and friends. It spoke of God's abundance, but it lacked mystery.

The Meaning of Christmas

According to the early church fathers, Christmas is more than lavish giving. Our worship bears a special, sacred character. To say the Christmas Eve service bears a special, sacred character points to the mystery of redemption that took place in the incarnation. Through the words and sensible signs done at the Christmas vigil, we tell and act out a mystery that touches the very meaning of human existence. Therefore, as we say and do this liturgy from the heart and mean what we hear, say, and do, God shapes us by the spiritual meaning of Christmas. In this service we not only celebrate Christ born in Bethlehem but Christ crucified, risen, and returning and Christ born in us. By opening our hearts and minds to the meaning of Christmas, it carries us into the reality that it signifies.

The church father who spoke most decisively and powerfully to the sacred nature of the Christmas Eve service is Leo, the Bishop of Rome (AD 440), who saw Christmas as not just a moving story but the starting point of our salvation. Christmas points to the paschal mystery, the Easter event to which it is already intricately bound. Consequently, Leo thought of Christmas as the "sacrament of the day of Christ's birth" and called upon us "to think of the Lord's birth, wherein the Word became Flesh, not as a past event which we recall, but as a present reality upon which we gaze" (italics added).[1] With this view of worship in mind, let me relate the content of the ancient Christmas Eve vigil and show how it celebrates the mystery of redemption that happened in history and now happens within us.

The first time I went to a Christmas Eve vigil, I did not realize I was stepping out of my usual way of celebrating Christmas and entering into a primal saving event in an experiential way. I thought I was simply going to another candlelight service, one that was more beautiful and more liturgical perhaps, but not one that was qualitatively different.

The Christmas Eve Vigil

The liturgical tradition, both Eastern and Western, is characterized by the belief that when we step into the sanctuary of the church, we have left earth and entered into the heavenly realm. I knew something was different as I took my seat in the near darkness of the sanctuary clutching the small candle given to me as I entered. As I sat there I could see the shadows of the mystery the church proclaims—the cross, the table of the Lord, the pulpit, the baptismal font, and the slightly arched curvature of the building that reached heavenward. Behind me I could hear the quiet footsteps and shuffling of the choir, acolytes, and ministers as they readied themselves for the procession. I closed my eyes and waited with curious anticipation for the service to begin. Everyone stood and I with them as we all turned toward the back of the church and spotted the members of the procession standing in the shadows.

A candle was lit, and a dim light barely stretched above the head of the celebrant and around the shoulders of the acolytes as well as several of the choir members in front. Then a clear piercing and haunting voice rang out: "Light and peace in Jesus Christ our Lord," and the congregation responded, strongly singing and proclaiming: "Thanks be to God." Then the organ, the stops out full, filled the sanctuary as we all sang the great Advent song:

> O come, O come Emmanuel,
> And ransom captive Israel,
> That mourns in lonely exile here
> Until the Son of God appear.
> Rejoice! rejoice! Emmanuel
> Shall come to thee, O Israel.[2]

As we sang this powerful prayer for Christ to come, the celebrants, acolytes, and choir processed. On their way they lit the candle of each person at the end of the pew, who in turn lit the candle of the person next to him or her and on down the pew. By the time the congregation arrived at the last verse, the processors were in their place of leadership. Trumpets then joined with the voices and organ to fill the place with the sounds of heaven. The bright light of all the candles filled the sanctuary with their light to make us feel as though we were standing in heaven itself around the dazzling throne of God as we sang one of the last verses:

> O come, Thou Key of David, come,
> And open wide our heavenly home;
> Make safe the way that leads on high,
> And close the path to misery.[3]

Then the leader, looking straight at us, declared in a strong, clear voice:

It is not ourselves we proclaim; we proclaim Christ Jesus as Lord, and ourselves as your servants, for Jesus' sake. For the same God who said, "Out of darkness let light shine," has caused his light to shine within us, to give the light of revelation—the revelation of the glory of God in the face of Jesus Christ.

2 Corinthians 4:5–6 NEB

Then, calling us to pray, the leader lifted his voice to heaven and approached God with these words: "O God, who hast caused this holy night to shine with the illumination of the true light: Grant us, we beseech thee, that as we have known the mystery of that light upon earth, so may we also perfectly enjoy him in heaven; where with thee and the Holy Spirit he liveth and reigneth, one God, in glory everlasting. Amen."[4]

Still standing, we responded to this opening Scripture and prayer by singing "Of the Father's Love Begotten."[5] We then listened to the reading of the Word of God interspersed by a psalm and the threefold alleluia: God comforts the people and calls on them to prepare for redemption (Isa. 40:1–11); in the fullness of time God sent God's child who is to reign forever and ever (Heb. 1:1–12); and the Word was made flesh, and we have seen the glory of God (John 1:1–18).

A sermon on the meaning of Christmas followed. After the creed a prayer was said, the peace was exchanged, and an anthem was sung. Then we celebrated the Eucharist. As I stepped out of the pew and walked toward the table to receive the bread and wine, I knew I was participating in an action that called me into the very heart of the faith itself, into the mystery of Christ born in my heart. This service was no mere intellectual recollection of a grand story but a sacred encounter with the babe born in Bethlehem. I was about to receive the child destined to give his life to defeat the power of evil in my life and in the world. As I lifted my hands to receive the bread of life and raised my mouth to meet the lowered chalice and receive the cup of salvation, the congregation was singing the moving Taize rendition of "Jesus, Remember Me When You Come into Your Kingdom." The crib and the cross met, and in the mystery of that moment I was touched by the grace of God who forgives our sins, heals our wounded lives, and calls us into hope. With the congregation I joined in the closing prayer with a renewed sense of its meaning:

> Almighty and everliving God,
> We thank you for feeding us with the spiritual food
> Of the most precious Body and Blood
> Of your Son our Savior Jesus Christ;
> And for assuring us in these holy mysteries
> That we are living members of the Body of Your Son,
> And heirs of your eternal kingdom.
> And now, Father, send us out
> To do the work you have given us to do,
> To love and serve you
> As faithful witnesses of Christ our Lord.
> To Him, To You, and To the Holy Spirit,
> Be honor and glory, now and forever. Amen.[6]

Themes of the Christmas Eve Vigil

What are the themes of this great service that forms our spirituality? First, it is of great significance that the Christmas vigil is at night. In the ancient church the night was not only for sleep but for contemplative prayer. Ancient Christians saw the night as the time to expect the Parousia (the second coming)—the time to long for Jesus' return to destroy the powers of evil and establish his kingdom over all the world. In Christian theology the night has always held special significance. The great events of redemption happen in the night: Israel's deliverance from Egypt, the institution of the Lord's Supper, the darkening of the world at the death of Jesus, the resurrection in the morning before dawn, and of course the birth of Jesus during the night.

Second, the lighting of candles in the Christmas Eve vigil speaks to an important theological conviction: The light bursts forth in the midst of the darkness to symbolize Christ, the light of the world. As St. John points out, "The light shines in the darkness, and the darkness has not overcome it" (John 1:5). And this light is Jesus, "The true light that enlightens every man" (John 1:9).

A third theme, already symbolized by the contrast between light and darkness, is the sense that the Advent expectation has been fulfilled. The Scripture readings and the prayers bring the worshiper into an encounter with the fulfillment of the Advent longing. Like the early Christian kerygma, this service proclaims the time has been fulfilled, the longing of Israel has been completed, the Messiah has arrived!

The spiritual stimulus of preparing for Christmas by keeping Advent makes Christmas considerably more spiritually satisfying. Christmas is approached with spiritual expectation. It becomes an occasion for a true experience of Christ being born anew in the world and in our hearts, calling us into a deeper commitment to become the new person Christ has called us to become and to live in the expectation of his return.

This call to commitment is stimulated by an encounter with the wonderful exchange, a fourth theme of the Christmas vigil. The ancient church marveled in the exchange that took place in the incarnation. The one who has been from before time becomes bound by time, space, and history. He becomes one of us so that we may become one with him.

Here, in the wonderful exchange that occurred in the incarnation, we touch on the matter that is of ultimate importance to our spirituality. For in this act we are moved to contemplate an unfathomable mystery—the mystery of our salvation, the mystery of our own person united with Christ and through Christ united with God.

Christmas Spirituality

At the heart of our Christmas spirituality is the mystery that God of very God became man of very man to destroy the power of evil and to restore creature and creation to God's intention for the world. Christmas as the fulfillment of our Advent expectation teaches that the work of restoring creation has begun.

Some modern theologians want to dismiss the incarnation as a myth. Incarnation, the liberals say, is one of the last of the Christian myths that needs to be deconstructed. We rid ourselves of the myth of Christ's presence in bread and wine in the sixteenth century; we overcame the myth of a divine Scripture in the eighteenth and nineteenth centuries. According to this view, the church has done very well without a supernatural view of the Eucharist and the Bible; thus, says this view, we ought to do equally well or better by demythologizing the idea that God actually became a man.

But in the early church it was believed as true, historical fact that God, the Holy One of Israel, the Creator and Sustainer of the universe, the one who lives in dazzling and eternal light, actually became a member of the human race through the birth of a virgin. He was, as St. Irenaeus wrote, "born by his own created order which he himself bears"[7] or, as a Christmas hymn in the Byzantine tradition proclaims, "today the virgin giveth birth to the transcendent in essence."[8]

The early church fathers loved to play with the paradox of God becoming human, for here in the mystery of the God-man is found the paradox of the universe. An ancient Orthodox prayer proclaims: "Today is born of the virgin him who holdest all creation in the hollow of his hand; He whose essence is untouchable is wrapped in swaddling clothes as a babe. The god who from of old established the heavens lieth in the manger. He who showered the people with manna in the wilderness feedeth on milk from the breasts. And the bridegroom of the church calleth the magi. And the son of the virgin accepteth gifts from them. We worship thy nativity, O Christ."[9]

As St. Gregory Nazianzus proclaimed in a sermon in AD 379, "Marvelous is the mystery proclaimed today: man's nature is made new as God becomes man; he remains what he was and becomes what he was not."[10] For early Christians the incarnation was no mythical idea akin to the stories of the Greek gods becoming men, nor was it a mere intellectual idea drawn from Greek philosophical concepts. It was instead a living reality indispensable to their spirituality. But what does the incarnation mean for our spirituality?

Primarily, the biblical-historical tradition teaches us that the incarnation is the starting point for our spirituality. In order to understand what this assertion means, let's look at the meaning of the incarnation more closely. The meaning is found in a paradox that sees the union between God and humans first from the God side, then from the human side. To summarize, God united himself with humans in order for men and women to be united with God. The incarnation is not something unrelated to us; it has everything to do with our spirituality—for the incarnation not only brings God to human nature but brings human nature to God.

Incarnational Spirituality: God United with Humans

The idea that spirituality begins in the contemplation of the incarnate Word is the theme of John's Gospel. We are called to an unceasing contemplation of the mystery of this unfathomable condescension. John tells us, "The Word became flesh and dwelt among us, full of grace and truth; we have beheld his glory, glory as of the only Son from the Father" (John 1:14). The key to the divine condescension is the "glory" of God that is seen in God's child.

In Israel the manifestation of God's glory is always associated with God's presence. The glory of God is always seen from a distance—the pillar of cloud by day and the pillar of fire by night (Exod. 13:21–22) or the glorious theophany when Israel entered into covenant with God: "thunders and lightnings, and a thick cloud upon the mountain, and a very loud trumpet blast, . . . Mount Sinai was wrapped in smoke, because the LORD descended upon it in fire" (Exod. 19:16, 18). Ezekiel also saw a vision of God's glory. He speaks of this vision with glowing images,

"Sapphire . . . gleaming bronze . . . appearance of fire . . . brightness round about . . . the appearance of the bow that is in the cloud on the day of rain . . . such was the appearance of the likeness of the glory of the LORD. And when I saw it, I fell upon my face" (Ezek. 1:26–28).

What Moses, the people of Israel, and the prophets saw veiled in splendor and dazzling array was the glory of God—the same glory we see in the face of the baby born in Bethlehem, for it is the glory of God that is fully present in Jesus, the incarnation of God. Consequently, in the Catholic liturgy of December 24, the entrance antiphon of the Christmas Eve vigil is appropriately, "Today you will know the Lord is coming, and in the morning you will see his glory."[11] The glory of God is that God has become united to human nature in order to unite human nature to God. In the incarnation, human nature—our human nature, the nature that we share with Jesus—was decisively united to God!

In order to understand how the union of the divine with the human in the God-man relates to our spirituality, we must see it in its larger cosmic sense: Because of sin, human nature has been separated from God by our own choice of the will. The first Adam has led us all into a breach with God—a breach that we have no power to restore. No human person no matter how contrite, how good, how moral and upright can restore men and women to fellowship and union with God. Because it was a human who broke the original relationship with God, the relationship with God had to be restored by a human. However, because no human has the power to restore that relationship, God became a man to restore our relationship with himself. This dealing of the relationship between humans and God became a reality in the incarnation when divine nature was united with the nature of humans. *What humans could not attain because they could not raise themselves to God, God attained by descending to humans.* In this divine action God's union with humans is manifest. Perhaps this is why the multitude of the heavenly host were heard at the birth of Christ praising God and saying, "Glory to God in the highest" (Luke 2:14).

There can be no such thing as spirituality without God initiating a relationship with human persons, a relationship that is traced back to the momentous event we celebrate as Christmas—God with us. But there is another side to spirituality that issues from the incarnation as well. That is the necessity of the human nature choosing to unite with God.

Incarnational Spirituality: Humans United with God

The divine side of the incarnation shows us that God indeed is the hound of heaven. God seeks us out. God initiates a relationship with us. The incarnation is the supreme example of this truth.

The other side of it is that the human will must respond to God. In the incarnation Jesus, who shares our human nature and our will, chooses to be united to God. The ancient monothelite controversy centered on the issue: Did Jesus have a human will? The controversy was answered with a *yes*. Jesus willed the union with God and willed throughout his life to be obedient to God's will for his life. From the human side, Jesus was no robot, no mere mechanical man who lived by an ironclad determinism. His human will was as real as ours, and by that will he had to make genuine choices. Jesus in his humanity fully chose to cooperate with the divine will. As a man he accomplished union with the Divine. He is the only man who has been united with the Divine, and he has done that for us all.

Here lies the other side of our spirituality. Even as Jesus willed to choose union with God in his life on earth, so we are called to unite our wills with the will of Jesus and through him be united to God.

We need to see this side of our spirituality in relationship to the larger picture. Even as Adam's nature was alienated from God because of sin, so Adam's will was separated from God because Adam chose to be in rebellion against God. In the incarnation Christ, who is the second Adam, repaired our nature and our will. Since he did this as a human being, we who share in the same humanity have the potential to live in union with God through Jesus Christ now in this life.

But how can we achieve union with God? Union with God proclaims the incarnation is achieved through the grace of God alone. We are embraced by God's grace and united to Christ.

The incarnation is an act of God's grace, as are the life of Christ, the cross, and the empty tomb. For by the grace of God poured out in these events, the possibility of overcoming our alienation from God is made available. We claim this grace, choose this grace, and enter into this grace by living in Jesus Christ.

Now the question is: How can we truly enter into this grace? What must the will do? In biblical language the will must be converted to Christ; it must put off the old person, which is fashioned according to the first Adam, and put on the new person, which is fashioned after the new Adam. So Paul writes, "Put to death therefore what is earthly in you: fornication, impurity, passion, evil desire, and covetousness, which is idolatry. . . . Put on the new nature, which is being renewed in knowledge after the image of its creator. . . . Put on then, as God's chosen ones, holy and beloved, compassion, kindness, lowliness, meekness, and patience" (Col. 3:5, 10, 12; see Col. 3:1–17). This Christlike orientation in life is the work of the Holy Spirit and is imaged by our identity with Christ in baptism.

Here Paul is describing an incarnational spirituality. The person whose life is "hid with Christ in God" (Col. 3:3) is renewed in the image of the Creator (Col. 3:10). Consequently the life that person now lives is a life in Christ, a life that expresses what it truly means to be in union with God through Christ by the Spirit.

Conversion and baptism signify our union with Jesus Christ. Baptism both announces the gospel and expresses our embrace of God's grace. In the first three centuries the church practiced baptism as the culminating act of the conversion process. After Constantine the church shifted to infant baptism. The desert fathers regarded infant baptism as a kind of hidden presence of God's grace awaiting the soul's desire. This beautiful image, which can also be applied to adult baptism, captures both the divine and human sides of our union with Christ. In the incarnation this perfect union between God and man is accomplished. In his death and resurrection, which are for us, he fulfills his incarnational intention. In baptismal spirituality we live out a life united with his humanity and through him are united to God.

Spiritual writers of the ancient tradition distinguish three stages people must make in the way of union: conversion of the will, liberation from the passions, and acquisition of that perfect love. The first stage, conversion of the soul, is rooted in repentance. Repentance is the act of turning away from our sinful condition, our conformity to the first Adam. But repentance in the ancient tradition is not a single, onetime act of turning away from sin. It is a constant, day-to-day, moment-by-moment turning from evil and turning to a life lived in union with God. Repentance is a continual return to our baptismal vows. Our Christmas spirituality, which we have identified as an incarnational spirituality, makes repentance possible. For God in the incarnation became one of us; he assumed our nature and our will and lived a life in our nature never choosing evil. Because of this victory over evil, Jesus makes it possible for us whose nature he shared to choose against the power of evil in our own lives. By the grace of the incarnation we can be converted to a new life in Christ. Because of the incarnation we can be cured.

The second stage, the liberation from the passions, is the condition of being cured. In the fourth-century debates about the incarnation, an axiom that guided the orthodox conclusions regarding the incarnation was "only that which God assumed became healed." If God in the incarnation had assumed the human nature but not the will, only the human nature would be cured. But because God assumed the human will, our human will may be cured through union with his human will. So Christ in the incarnation liberates the passions and frees them from their imprisonment to the first Adam. One who turns to Christ in continual repentance may be continually freed from the passions and lusts of the flesh and evil desires. When we turn away from something, we turn toward something new. We turn toward the new life in Christ. We replace the old habits and old ways of life with new habits and new ways of life. We become new persons. We are born anew and become new creatures in Christ (2 Cor. 5:17). We now "walk by the Spirit, and do not gratify the desires of the flesh." And "the fruit of the Spirit is love, joy, peace, patience, kindness, goodness, faithfulness, gentleness, self-control" (Gal. 5:16, 22–23; see Gal. 5:16–24).

It is this transition from the old to the new that brings us into the third stage of spiritual progress, an acquisition of that perfect love in union with God. Our human nature has the possibility of being united with God through prayer because Christ unites his human nature with God.

The prayer that brings about union with God is not the active prayer of petitions and requests. It is the contemplative prayer, the prayer of a heart that is fully open to God. In the prayer of the heart we contemplate the world that will come and call upon God to empower that world now in the way we live. In this way we keep the Pauline admonition to "set your minds on things that are above, not on things that are on the earth" (Col. 3:2). The heart is the center that radiates to the whole person. It is open to the permeating presence of God so that as the ancient fathers taught, the person grasping the blessedness of the age to come will be formed into the image of Christ.

The desert fathers called it the Jesus Prayer and regarded its most basic element as the frequent repetition of the name of the Lord. In the *Philocalie* the story is told that when Abbot Macarius was asked how to pray, he answered, "There is no need to waste time with words: it is enough to hold out your hands and say, Lord, according to your desire and to your wisdom, have mercy. If you are hard pressed in the struggle, say: Lord, save me! He knows what is best for you, and he will have mercy on you."[12]

This method of prayer was to speak, "Lord Jesus Christ, Son of God, have mercy upon me, a sinner," until the prayer was continuous with the beat of the heart and brought the person into quiet rest in Jesus.

Our whole life is to be a life of prayer, a life of continual turning to God, and a life of reliance, faith, and trust in the living God. It is the continuousness of the Jesus Prayer that keeps us in this state of perpetual relationship to God. If you have never said this prayer, I recommend it to you. When you awake in the morning, when you drive in your car, when you are relaxed in the privacy of your home or place of retreat, or when you lie down at night say over and over again, "Lord Jesus Christ, Son of God, have mercy upon me, a sinner." Although this prayer was at one time the exclusive possession of the monastics, an anonymous writing of the nineteenth century known as *The Way of the Pilgrim* has shown how this prayer can be at the center of the life of any person who commits to live in the presence of God, in the glory of God revealed in Jesus Christ.

Finally, the union with God achieved through prayer results in the fruit of love. Love is the gift of the Holy Spirit. Incarnational love is, as the early church taught, "the very life of the divine nature." Here the effect of the incarnation is working in us. For the gift of God at Christmas communicates the divine nature to us truly and effectively. We receive this gift when we choose to follow the path of repentance, conversion, the turning away from the passions, and acquisition of love. This fundamental unity with God through love evidences itself through the love of neighbor, which is the love Jesus himself showed in his self-giving. For the one who came at Christmas came not to rule over earthly kingdoms through political power. Rather, he came to serve humanity, to give his life as a ransom for many.

This understanding of spirituality is rooted in the classical biblical and historical view of God incarnate in Jesus Christ, the mystery of salvation we celebrate at the Christmas Eve vigil. A theology that ignores the dimension of incarnational spirituality has lost touch with ancient spirituality and an essential feature of Christianity. It no longer has the power to help us understand and live by the healing touch brought to our lives by the God who became one of us in the womb of the virgin and was born of her in Bethlehem of Judea.

Living an Incarnational Spirituality

As I stated earlier, the incarnation is not a mere dry, intellectual idea that belongs to the realm of metaphysics. Instead it is a living reality that has the power to shape our spirituality and direct us in becoming new creatures in Christ.

Paul's Understanding of Incarnational Spirituality

The apostle Paul understood the practical spiritual impact of the incarnation and applied it to a situation in the Philippian church. By looking at this example we may gain an understanding of how the incarnation is to work in our own lives.

When Paul wrote to the Philippians, one of his major concerns was a rift in the church. Apparently there were two factions in the church led by two women: "I entreat Euodia and I entreat Syntyche to agree in the Lord" (Phil. 4:2). Here Paul is begging them to come to a cease-fire and to work together in harmony in the body of Christ. But this appeal must not be seen in isolation from the larger context. Space does not permit a complete evaluation of the book, so let it be sufficient to say that Paul's appeal is in light of the incarnation as expressed in the hymn in chapter 2. He introduces the hymn by saying, "Let each of you look not only to his own interests, but also to the interests of others" (Phil. 2:4). Then he calls on them:

> Have this mind [that is, the incarnation] among yourselves, which is yours in Christ Jesus, who, though he was in the form of God, did not count equality with God a thing to be grasped, but emptied himself, taking the form of a servant, being born in the likeness of men. And being found in human form he humbled himself and became obedient unto death, even death on a cross. Therefore God has highly exalted him and bestowed on him the name which is above every name, that at the name of Jesus every knee should bow, in heaven and on earth and under the earth, and every tongue confess that Jesus Christ is Lord, to the glory of God the Father.
>
> Philippians 2:5–11

What Paul was saying to them and to us is something like this: "To be in Christ means you must live in an incarnational way, putting yourself in the other person's shoes." Incarnational living is a difficult assignment. It was for Euodia and Syntyche in the first century and it is equally difficult for us today in the twenty-first century. We can come up with so many objections: "But what about *my* point of view?" Or, "I'll be nothing but a doormat for people to walk on." Regardless, the message is clear: "Do not make your main concern that of looking out for yourself. Rather, be like Jesus and always be concerned for the well-being of the other." This is incarnational spirituality. It is the humility of life by which Christmas calls us to live.

Christmas Examples of Incarnational Spirituality

The biblical themes chosen for reading during the Christmas season have as their underlying concern the continuation of the incarnation in the lives of God's people. At first glance the three feast days right after Christmas seem curiously out of keeping with the Christmas season—St. Stephen, St. John, and the slaughter of the holy innocents. However, here we have three examples of humility—persons who put their concern for others before their concern for self. Stephen, the first martyr of the church, did not defend himself when he was brought before the council and falsely charged with teaching blasphemy (Acts

6:13). Instead he proclaimed Christ, the message that was burning in his heart (Acts 7), and he was stoned to death in the sight of many, including Saul, who was later to become Paul the missionary (Acts 7:58).

That we are called to live a life for the sake of others was clearly expressed in the writings of St. John the Evangelist. His purpose in life was not to serve himself but to serve the mission of Jesus. He turned people toward the Word who "became flesh and made his dwelling among us" and we have seen the glory, not of St. John, but his glory "who came from the Father" (John 1:14 NIV).

This theme of an incarnational spirituality is also present in the holy innocents. Even though they had little conscious choice in the matter, they gave up their innocent lives for the sake of the gospel and became a prototype of the martyrs of the church (Matt. 2:16–18).

Our Christmas Calling: Humility of Life

In light of the incarnation and the incarnational spirituality it calls us to follow, it seems appropriate that we should use this season as a time to meditate and act on the virtue of humility. Before we can ask what it means for us to live out an incarnational humility, we need to examine ourselves for the presence of the opposite.

The opposite of humility is vanity. In vanity we look to ourselves rather than to God. We give ourselves credit for our talents, abilities, insights, accomplishments, looks, and position in society. We refuse to admit we are indebted to others, to God's grace, to a fortunate birth, to a privileged education, or to the interest others have taken in us. Consequently we fail to be grateful to those who have helped us attain or achieve our privileges. Vanity produces hypocrisy; we pretend to have virtues we do not possess. Vanity also leads to fake humility and to a judgmental attitude, often judging in others what we excuse in ourselves. Vanity expresses itself in boastful talk, exaggeration of the truth, drawing attention to self, and claiming abilities, wisdom, experience, and influence we don't have. Vanity produces eccentric behavior, tantrums, pouting, and manipulation to get what we want. Vanity also seeks to impress others with power, money, expensive surroundings, and material wealth and always looks for flattery and compliments.

The opposite of humility is also arrogance. Arrogant people insist on others conforming to their wishes and plans. They demand other people recognize their leadership, and they act in an overbearing, argumentative, opinionated, and obstinate way. Arrogance also breeds snobbery. A snob is proud about things such as race, family, and personality and is given to flaunt his or her position, education, skill, or possessions.

As I pray through the above description of vanity and arrogance, I find myself described more times than I would wish. I recognize that my commitment to Christ calls me into union with the human nature and the human will I share with Christ, who became a human being so I might become like him and acquire within my own person the characteristics of the new person. One of these virtues, the one we have chosen to meditate on during the Christmas season, is the virtue of humility. God calls us to enter into the spirit of this season by entering into Christ in such a way that we live out his humility.

Humility requires that we put off our vanity, our arrogance, and our snobbery. In its place we are to put on Christ, to "do nothing from selfishness or conceit, but in humility count others better than yourselves" (Phil. 2:3). We are to come to Jesus and as he commanded, "Take my yoke upon you, and learn from me; for I am gentle and lowly in heart, and you will find rest for your souls" (Matt. 11:29). For "God opposes the proud, but gives grace to the humble" (James 4:6).

Next God calls on us to take on a humiliation. Some time ago I was having lunch with one of my older students who takes a course or two every semester while working as a night janitor in one of the college buildings. As customary I inquired about his background. Much to my surprise I discovered that he had an M.A. in engineering and once owned a prosperous business, which he sold and then became a highly successful insurance broker. "John," I asked, "why are you sweeping buildings?" "Because I want to learn humility and some day serve our Lord on the mission field." The early church fathers frequently counseled people to learn humility by taking on a humiliation.

St. Bernard is rumored to have said, "He is humble who converts humiliations into humility." As long as we feel humiliated we are not perfectly humble. To choose a humiliation is to choose a grace that will produce the fruit of humility.

There is great value in humility, but it is not a value that should fill us with pride. Humility is a powerful weapon against the devil, for he cannot defend himself against it; it is a source of strength, for it calls us to abandon ourselves to God. Humility provides us with courage to undertake great things because our trust is not in self but in God. Humility makes all things possible; it fills us with love; and it makes us see our own faults and not those of others.

The attainment of humility is a grace, a gift from God. When we encounter it in Christ, the source of this grace, we must cooperate with it and choose it. We must pray for the grace of humility and accept humiliations when they come our way. We are to keep our minds off the faults of others and see ourselves as we really are. And we ought not to seek praise for our good works.

Finally, the early fathers taught that humility is the foundation of all the virtues and works within us that true spirit of meekness Christ called us to express in our lives. As we allow ourselves to be formed by the incarnation, the self-emptying of the Son of God shines through our words and actions.

Conclusion

So how does the Christmas season shape our personal and congregational spirituality? On paper, it looks so very simple—live the incarnate life in union with Jesus. But in reality the challenge to the incarnate life, that life in union with God, is a profound emptying of self to become one in life with Jesus the incarnate God. Christmas spirituality acknowledges that your life in God is a gift of union with Jesus Christ and the calling to bring your life into his life. This mystery is expressed in the ancient Christmas vigil, continues in the contemplation of your identity with God incarnate in continual repentance and prayer, and manifests itself in the humility of your spirit and life lived among others. Christmas calls us to this kind of incarnational spirituality, a spirituality achieved wholly in Jesus, given to us as a gift, and lived out by us through the choices we make. In this way Christmas becomes a time when Jesus who was born in Bethlehem is born in our lives.

Table 4: A Summary of Christmas Spirituality

Theme	Spiritual Emphasis
What is the meaning of Christmas?	"Think of the Lord's birth, wherein the Word became Flesh, not as a past event which we recall, but as a *present reality* upon which we gaze" (St. Leo, AD 440).
What is the Christmas Eve service?	More than an observation, it is to be a participation in the incarnation event. It is in the *night*, the time of God's great redemptive acts. The *light* of the candles symbolizes the bursting forth of the light of Christ in a dark world. Christ calls us to live in expectation of his return.
What is Christmas spirituality?	The mystery that God became a man, that by man united to God he might defeat the powers of darkness.
What is incarnational spirituality?	The mystery of humanity united to God. Because Jesus was united to God, we, through our union with Jesus in faith signified by baptism, are united with God.

What are the ancient steps that speak to our union with God?	Step 1. Conversion and continual repentance. Step 2. Liberation of the passions from the first Adam. Step 3. Continuous prayer.
How do we *live* incarnational spirituality?	The life of incarnational spirituality is that of emptying oneself.
Name three examples of incarnational spirituality celebrated in the Christmas season.	The martyrdom of Stephen The beheading of John the Baptist The slaughter of the holy innocents
What posture should we adopt to live incarnational spirituality?	Humility Take on a humiliation Seek meekness

A PRAYER FOR CHRISTMAS

Almighty God, you have given your only begotten Son to take our nature upon him, and to be born [this day] of a pure virgin; grant that we, who have been born again and made your children by adoption and grace, may daily be renewed by your Holy Spirit; through our Lord Jesus Christ, to whom with you and the same Spirit be honor and glory, now and forever. Amen.

From *The Book of Common Prayer*

Questions for Reflection

1. Is the birth of Christ a present, daily reality in your life?
2. How do you connect the dots between the incarnation and the death and resurrection?
3. What words or images do you use to grasp the significance of God's union with our human nature so that, through our union with Jesus, we are united to God the Father by the work of the Spirit?
4. How do you find yourself living out the reality of an incarnational spirituality?
5. How do you feel about the fact that Stephen, John the Baptist, and the holy innocents are used as examples of incarnational spirituality during the Christmas season?
6. Are you willing to take on a humiliation to experience incarnational spirituality? What might that be?

Resources for Christmas Worship and Preaching

See Robert Webber, ed., *The Services of the Christian Year*, vol. 5 of *The Complete Library of Christian Worship* (Peabody, MA: Hendrickson, 1994), 157–208.

- Introduction to Christmas worship
- Resources for planning Christmas worship
- The arts for Christmas worship
- Sample services for Christmas worship

EPIPHANY

A Time to Manifest Christ

Stars cross the sky, wise men journey from pagan lands, earth receives its savior in a cave. Let there be no one without a gift to offer, no one without gratitude as we celebrate the salvation of the world, the birthday of the human race. Now it is no longer, "dust you are and to dust you shall return," but "you are joined to heaven and into heaven shall you be taken up."

Basil the Great (AD 330–379)

All of us at one time or another have experienced an unusual event, an event that has presented us with an insight, a revelation, or a manifestation. These events are glimpses into something beyond the ordinary, invitations to see a reality that lies behind the humdrum of the usual. Epiphany is that kind of event.

In the Christian Scriptures the word *epiphany* is used three times by Paul. Two of the references speak of the second coming: "awaiting our blessed hope, the appearing *(epiphanian)* of the glory of our great God and Savior Jesus Christ" (Titus 2:13; see also 2 Thess. 2:8). The third time the word *epiphany* appears, the reference is to the first coming of Christ: "the grace which [God] . . . now has manifested through the appearing *(epiphaneias)* of our Savior Christ Jesus, who abolished death and brought life and immortality to light through the gospel" (2 Tim. 1:9–10).

In the early church the feast of Epiphany originally celebrated the birth of Christ. However, after the birth of Christ was placed on December 25 to replace the pagan feast of the birth of the sun, Epiphany was designated as the event that manifested Jesus as the Son of God, the Savior of the world. In the East, Epiphany was appointed as the day to celebrate the baptism of Jesus. However, in the West, Epiphany became the day to celebrate the manifestation of Jesus through three great events: the visit of the Magi, the baptism of Jesus, and the marriage feast of Cana.

Today Epiphany brings us to the end of the Christmas cycle, completing the great rhythm of expectation and fulfillment that defines this period of time. It also points to the beginning of Christ's manifestation to the world, a ministry that not only happened in the first century but happens now within the church and within us as we travel through the unfolding of the paschal mystery of the liturgical year.

The Epiphany Service

In the liturgical calendar Christmas is not over until January 5, the eve of Epiphany. However, in our civil calendar Christmas is behind us after December 25. The new year has begun, and we are already off onto new things. Unfortunately, for this reason Epiphany and the impact it can make on our spiritual pilgrimage does not receive the attention it deserves. Epiphany is much more than an interesting story about three Magi, for through this event we are to experience a manifestation of our own spirituality.

The Three Wise Men

In the Western church January 6, the day of Epiphany, is always a celebration of the coming of the wise men who brought gold, frankincense, and myrrh to Jesus. Certainly it is a fair question to ask what value these stories offer to our spiritual journey today in the twenty-first century. If we are to penetrate into the very heart of Epiphany, to the very soul of its meaning for us, we need to do more than hear the Scripture account of the Magi. We also need to participate in a meditative way in the entire service of worship into which this story has been placed because this piece of the unfolding mystery of salvation is the key to the shape of our spiritual experience between now and Lent. Even as our Christmas spirituality was shaped by the dominant theme of the incarnation, so now our Epiphany spirituality will be shaped by the overriding theme of Christ's manifestation as Savior of the world. Even as the incarnation finds its continuation *in us* through our union with Christ, so the Epiphany of Christ is extended *in us* through the practice of Epiphany spirituality. Our Epiphany journey can start at no better place than the Epiphany service of worship.

The first time I went to an Epiphany service I was not certain what to expect. Having been raised in a nonliturgical tradition, I didn't know the meaning of the word *epiphany*. But I looked it up and discovered it meant "an appearance or manifestation, especially of a divine being." It was also interesting for me to discover the word had special meaning in the ancient world because it was used to describe the appearance of a ruler. The same culture that birthed the Bible and the early church celebrated the visit of its ruler with great pomp and circumstance. The ruler's visit was always a lavish affair marked by feasting and a celebrative mood. I assumed the service was going to celebrate the Epiphany, the appearance of Jesus, and do so in a lavish fashion. I was disappointed that there were only a few people present and that the service wasn't nearly as lavish in ceremony as I expected. (This is now changing as churches are once again stressing the importance of Epiphany to our spiritual lives.) Nevertheless, I was gratified by the content of the service and the stimulus it gave me toward an Epiphany spirituality. Let me share it with you.

I was immediately drawn up into the meaning of the service and into the place it played in the unfolding drama of the mystery of salvation as we stood to sing:

> What star is this, with beams so bright,
> more beauteous than the noonday light?
> It shines to herald for a king,
> and Gentiles to his crib to bring.[1]

Again, the meaning of why I was there struck my mind and heart as the minister prayed: "O God, who by the leading of a star didst manifest Thy only begotten Son to the peoples of the earth: Lead us, who know Thee now by faith, to Thy presence, where we may behold Thy glory face to face; through the same Jesus Christ our Lord, who liveth and reigneth with Thee and the Holy Spirit, one God, now and forever. Amen."[2]

The star that was to lead me that night was this service of worship. It was the star that would take me by the hand to kneel by the crib of the one I met at Christmas and acknowledged by faith to be the Son of God. But the purpose of this encounter was to take me more deeply into the mystery, to bring me face-to-face with the child who would be manifested not only in me but also to the whole world. With others I prayed, "Oh Lord, open my heart and mind to you and prepare me to be in your presence and behold your glory."

Then we sat to hear the Scripture. The Scriptures that day and at every Epiphany celebration are the same: Isaiah 60:1–6, 9; Psalm 72; Ephesians 3:1–12; and, of course, the story of the Magi, Matthew 2:1–12. Read in this order, they all fit with the prayer for the day and fulfill the prayer's promise that "we may behold Thy glory face to face." A few brief comments on the meaning of the texts will point to the glory of God, once seen as a distant threat on the holy mountain, now present in Jesus Christ and through him available as a personal presence to all the peoples of the world.

These texts speak of the fulfillment of prophecy. The prophecy is that the once distant glory of God will become a presence to the whole world. The Epiphany marks the turning point of the prophecy. The glory of God that has become incarnate is now manifested to the Magi, who represent the peoples of the world beyond Israel. From them the manifest glory of God will extend through the church to the whole world.

The Scriptures taken as a whole appear like an hourglass set on its side. The left side of the hourglass contains the prophecies of Isaiah and the psalmist who proclaim the coming Epiphany. The reading from Matthew stands at the center in the funnel of the hourglass representing the arrival of the promise. And the right side of the hourglass represents the text from Ephesians, which describes the work of the church as the calling to manifest the Christ to the whole world. The glory of God has come to earth and will spread throughout the universe! This is the shout of Epiphany, the cry that is to grasp our hearts and give us hope because we have gazed into the face of God's glory. A few comments about the texts will help us see the reality Epiphany proclaims.

Look at the Gospel story of the Magi, which only Matthew tells. The story fits comfortably with Matthew's purpose in writing the Gospel. His overriding theme is the fulfillment of prophecy in Jesus Christ and the establishment of his kingdom throughout the world. The story of the Magi fulfills the promise that the light of Christ will extend to the whole world, with the Magi representing nations outside of Israel who come to worship Christ as their king.

The Epiphany theme, so close to the heart of Matthew, was a divisive issue in the primitive Christian community. Even the disciples had to be persuaded that Christ's coming was not only to Israel but to the whole world (see Acts 10:1–11:18). When Matthew wrote the Gospel and directed it to the Jewish community, he had this axe to grind. Not only did Christ come as the fulfillment of Jewish prophecy, he came to be the Savior of the whole world, not just the Jews. This message was not readily accepted because it went against the grain of Jewish exclusiveness.

The Old Testament readings for Epiphany support this radical concept of the universalized manifestation of the glory of God, the availability of Jehovah's glory to all the nations of the earth. What was once the exclusive possession of Israel now belongs to the world, to all people, to the Gentiles. So Isaiah prophesied:

> Arise, shine; for your light has come, and the glory of the LORD has risen upon you. For behold, darkness shall cover the earth, and thick darkness the peoples; but the LORD will arise upon you, and his glory will be seen upon you. And nations shall come to your light, and kings to the brightness of your rising.

Isaiah 60:1–3

The message of Psalm 72 also emphasizes the universal nature of Christ's mission to the world: "May the kings of Tarshish and of the isles render him tribute, may the kings of Sheba and Seba bring gifts! May all kings fall down before him, all nations serve him!" (vv. 10–11).

While the Old Testament lessons proclaim the prophecy and Matthew describes the fulfillment of the prophecy in Christ, the Epistle declares how the nations of the earth will hear of Christ, the light of the world: "This grace was given, to preach to the Gentiles the unsearchable riches of Christ, and to make all men see what is the plan of the mystery hidden for ages in God who created all things; that through the church the manifold wisdom of God might now be made known" (Eph. 3:8–10).

The church is the sign of Christ in the world—the continuing manifestation of Jesus in the world. The church is not primarily a building, diocese, or denomination but a people. I am the church; you are the church.

As I listened to these passages and to their explanation, I realized that an epiphany was occurring for me right there in the service of worship. I was seeing the glory of God in Christ face-to-face. This manifestation, this epiphany, was not to be a thing of the past, something that happened two thousand years ago, but was to be an appearance *now* in the body of Christ assembled, an epiphany *in me*. I had been called from light to darkness, and now I was to be a manifestation of Christ. My part was to respond, to say *yes* to the calling, to commit my life to be a center through which the Epiphany could be extended beyond the crib to the world of my everyday experience.

As the Epiphany continued to press itself upon me during the creed, the prayers, the peace, and the Eucharist, I found myself fighting the call to an Epiphany spirituality. I wanted to treat the service like a play to be observed. "The incarnation is for me," I thought, "but the Epiphany is for others. It's for the pastor, the evangelists, the missionaries. They have been called to an Epiphany spirituality. But God doesn't need me to be an epiphany."

This is a tension all of us experience. We struggle with the mandate to be a witness to Christ in our everyday working lives, and many of us shun it, hiding our light under a bushel. But the mission of the church and of every member of Christ's body is a mandate that cannot be denied. We are his body, the church. And the church is a movement sent on a mission by God—a mission that involves us all. More about this later.

After Epiphany

The service of January 6 touches us with the very heart of Epiphany and calls us to practice an Epiphany spirituality. Then our experience after the Epiphany season continues to be enriched and challenged by two other great mysteries that Epiphany celebrates: the baptism of Jesus and the marriage feast in Cana of Galilee.

The Baptism of Jesus

The baptism of Jesus, which is celebrated on the first Sunday after Epiphany, holds significant meaning for our own spirituality because it takes us more deeply into the paschal mystery, the source of our spirituality. The theme of Jesus' baptism is that salvation is extended to all people, that sin is under an ultimate judgment, and that Jesus is proclaimed God's Son, the Lamb of God who removes sin, the one anointed to be the Messianic King. For these reasons ancient Christianity celebrates the baptism of our Lord as a major feast, the primary Epiphany of Christ. Indeed, the baptism of our Lord receives more frequent attention in ancient iconography than many other events in the life of Christ!

Unfortunately, for many Christians the celebration of the baptism of Jesus is just another event that passes by without much personal attention other than the recalling of a unique experience in the life of Christ. In our spiritual pilgrimage God calls us to break through a passive spirit concerning the baptism of Jesus and recover the full meaning of this event for our own spirituality. For the baptism of Jesus is not only an event that happened to Jesus but one that happens to us. It defines our spirituality and gives impetus to the kind of people we are to become.

Like all the other events in the life of Jesus, the baptism of our Lord is replete with imagery expressing powerful insight into the meaning of our own spirituality. One of the most prominent images is the Jordan River itself.

The early church fathers saw the Jordan as a type of our own baptism. Like the Red Sea, the Jordan symbolizes an important passage in the life of Israel. The people of Israel passed through the waters of Jordan and left their wilderness wanderings behind as they entered God's Promised Land. Jordan is a water of passage. The symbol implies movement from one condition to another.

The baptism by John in the river Jordan was a special turning point in Jesus' life, turning from a time of obscurity into a time to manifest himself as the Son of God who had come to take away the sins of the world. When we celebrate the baptism of Jesus, then, we not only celebrate his baptism but also the meaning of baptism for us.

To grasp the meaning of what we do when we celebrate the baptism of Jesus we must first sense what the baptism meant for Jesus and then ask what it means for us today. First, Jesus was baptized *for the sins of the people for whom he was going to die.* The baptism and the cross are connected—the real meaning of the baptism is in the paschal mystery. This interpretation was affirmed by John in what must have been a startling revelation to his hearers: "Behold, the Lamb of God, who takes away the sin of the world!" (John 1:29). In these words John was articulating a reality that he himself experienced. He already knew several things when Jesus came to be baptized by him. He knew someone was to come after him who was mightier and more important than himself (Matt. 3:11–12), and he knew from Isaiah that the Spirit would descend and rest on the Messiah (Isa. 11:1–2; John 1:32–33). Consequently, because of the symbols attending Jesus' baptism, John could say with confidence, "This is the Son of God" (John 1:34).

The key to John's enlightenment and to our understanding of how baptism and the cross come together is caught in the word *lamb.* Surely John the Baptist, being a Jew, had in mind the meaning attached to *lamb* in Jewish religious thought. Jesus as the Lamb of God calls to mind the Passover lamb of Exodus 12, whose annual immolation at the Passover festival had an expiatory function. Jesus is the Lamb who has come to make expiation for the sin of the world; the one being baptized is also the one who will die to make atonement for all the people of the world. But also, John may have had in mind the suffering servant of Yahweh described in Isaiah 53:7: "He was oppressed, and he was afflicted, yet he opened not his mouth; like a lamb that is led to the slaughter, and like a sheep that before its shearers is dumb, so he opened not his mouth."

These words refer to Isaiah 53:4 and the Lamb who bears our infirmities or to Exodus 12:23 and the Passover lamb whose blood, in the Christian interpretation, takes away sins. Thus John the Baptist, interpreted by St. John the Gospel writer, may very well be revealing the manifestation that Jesus is not only the "beloved Son" (Matt. 3:17) but also the Christ who is to be "our Passover" (1 Cor. 5:7 NIV).

Second, if it is true that Jesus was baptized for those for whom he would die, then it is essential for us to ask, what does Jesus' baptism mean for me? What should be the effect on me of the worship that celebrates the baptism of Jesus in the Jordan?

Epiphany worship never allows us to be a mere observer of what is taking place. Epiphany is not a play or a drama that we nonchalantly gaze on from a distance. No, the liturgy calls us to enter into the drama as players, to be there as participants, to let happen in our hearts and minds what is being done in the words and actions of the liturgy. So how are we to enter into the baptism of Jesus? St. Gregory of Nyssa, an Eastern father of the fourth century, answers that question this way: "Leave the desert, that is to say, sin. Cross the Jordan. Hasten toward life according to Christ, toward the earth which bears the fruits of joy, where run, according to the promise, streams of milk and honey. Overthrow Jericho, the old dwelling place, do not leave it fortified. All these things are a figure of ourselves. All are prefiguration of realities which are now made manifest."[3]

First, as Christ was baptized to destroy all evil, so the baptism of Jesus calls on us to flee all darkness. If we are to fulfill the meaning of Jesus' baptism in our own lives, we need to make it an occasion for self-examination. Because we wrestle against principalities and powers, the power of evil is always there, relentlessly working to capture our attention and commitment. But because Christ was baptized *for us* and *for our sin*, his baptism, which was fulfilled in the cross, can be an occasion for us to put to death the evil powers of the underworld that call us into their service.

But second, the putting down of evil is only one side of Christ's work for us. He was baptized and died not only to put away evil but to restore the world and us, his people. To be in Christ is to be a new creation (2 Cor. 5:17). We enter into the new community that constitutes the beginning again of the created order. Consequently, the baptism of Jesus is an occasion for us to commit ourselves once again to the process of becoming a new person. What choices must we make to put the old person behind and allow the new person formed in the image of Christ to emerge?

Finally, as Christ received the Spirit at baptism, the Spirit that came upon him to empower him to do the work God called him to do, so the celebration of the baptism of Jesus is an occasion for us to receive in a new and fresh way the Spirit that enlightens our understanding and empowers us to proclaim with John, "Behold, the Lamb of God, who takes away the sin of the world!" (John 1:29). When we are able to confess these words in our hearts and express them on our lips and in our lives, the baptism of Jesus is no longer a thing outside of our experience but a vital and living expression of an Epiphany spirituality we own. For the Spirit who came upon him and said, "This is my beloved Son" (Matt. 3:17), has come upon us and claims us as a child of God, a member of the community for whom Jesus was baptized.

The Wedding Feast in Cana

Another special feast to celebrate during the after Epiphany season is the wedding feast in Cana, a manifestation of Christ we recall every third year on the second Sunday after Epiphany (John 2:1–11). The wedding feast, like the other events in the life of Christ, is not an isolated episode but one with an ultimate meaning found in the paschal mystery. Here the glory of God comes down from the mountain and is manifested in something as common as a wedding party. If we are to know the meaning of this feast for our own spirituality we must ask, what does the feast mean for Jesus, and how can we experience its meaning in our own lives?

First, the key to the primary meaning this feast held for Jesus may be found in the complicated and controversial words, "My hour has not yet come" (John 2:4). This phrase, a favorite of St. John's, is found frequently in his Gospel:

"No one laid hands on him, because his hour had not yet come" (John 7:30, see also 8:20).

"The hour has come for the Son of man to be glorified" (John 12:23).

"Now is my soul troubled. And what shall I say? 'Father, save me from this hour'? No, for this purpose I have come to this hour. Father, glorify thy name" (John 12:27–28).

"Now before the feast of the Passover, when Jesus knew that his hour had come to depart out of this world to the Father" (John 13:1).

"Father, the hour has come; glorify thy Son that the Son may glorify thee" (John 17:1).

In these passages the word *hour* is clearly associated with the death of Jesus, the paschal mystery. But why did Jesus use the word at the marriage feast?

It is generally agreed that the answer to this question is not found in the text itself but in the larger context of John's Gospel. The whole Gospel appears to be a progressive manifestation of the glory of Jesus, a catechesis of the early church that moves out of the text, "and the Word became flesh and dwelt among us . . . ; we have beheld his glory" (John 1:14). The ultimate glory of God is in Christ crucified and risen for the salvation of the world, the message that John progressively unfolds. Thus the marriage feast of Cana is one of the events in a long chain of manifestations leading to the ultimate revelation of God's glory in the paschal mystery. Consequently, while the full hour of God's glory to be revealed in Christ had not yet come, an insight into his glory came when he turned water into wine. So John could say of this miracle, "This, the first of his signs, Jesus did at Cana in Galilee, and *manifested his glory;* and his disciples believed in him" (John 2:11, italics added).

The fathers of the early church loved to comment on the rich symbolism of this story as they searched for profound liturgical and spiritual meanings. Water prefigures baptism and the change that comes into the life of the believer; it symbolizes the cup of Jesus' passion and death; it is a sign of the Eucharist that makes Christ present in the symbol of wine; and it is a type of the messianic banquet at the end of history when the nations will gather at the wedding feast of the Lamb.

Clearly the fathers saw a connection between Cana and all the mysteries of life present in the cross, the resurrection, the church, and the new creation of the end time. And in this they point to the true meaning of the wedding feast for us. It points to the ultimate meaning of life in Christ and calls us to a spirituality that centers in the pattern of the old made new. Even as Jesus turned water into wine, so he is able to take our lives and transform them into new wine to his glory. As we enter into the meaning of this celebration, the question for us is how thoroughly we are willing to let the one who can turn water into wine turn our lives away from the power of darkness toward new goals and aspirations, goals of the kingdom, goals of the new person in Christ. God wants to make us an epiphany of his glory. But he can only do that if we cooperate with his Spirit and turn our lives over to him without reservation or equivocation.

The After Epiphany Season Theme

The theme of the entire Epiphany season is the glory of God manifested through Jesus. The glory, which for the Jewish people was only a distant reality, has now become a visible, tangible, walking, feeling, touching member of the human race. This glory, revealed at the birth of Christ and known to the Magi, was largely hidden from the people until it was powerfully revealed at the baptism of Jesus and partially manifested at the wedding feast. This glory will be revealed again in all its power in the paschal mystery and again at the second coming of Christ. In the meantime, between the wedding feast in Cana and the impending death of Jesus, a progressive unveiling of his glory will appear. The season after Epiphany to the beginning of Lent (known as ordinary time) celebrates this progressive unveiling of God's glory manifest in Jesus and invites us to order our spiritual journey around the Christ manifest in history, manifest in us. The after Epiphany themes of God's glory manifest in Jesus include the calling of the disciples, their training, the exhibiting of his powers, rejection by his own people, and in the final week of the after Epiphany season, the transfiguration.

Calling the Disciples

Calling the disciples and gathering a band of followers around himself seems like a very natural thing for Jesus to do. Although practical, it was also an activity with important theological overtones. Jesus was gathering to himself the band of people who would act as a sign and witness to the glory of God manifest in Jesus, for in them and through them the glory of God would continue to be manifest throughout the world. In the season after Epiphany Christ calls us through the liturgy to become his disciples, to follow after him, and to manifest his glory through our own lives.

The stories told by the Gospel writers to convey the calling of the disciples contain some very thoughtful insights on discipleship—perspectives that help us understand the meaning of our own spirituality today. First, the call of discipleship appears to be a mutual discovery. John relates the call of Andrew and Peter (John 1:35–42), who were disciples of John the Baptist. John the Baptist, seeking nothing for himself, readily gave up his own disciples when he pointed Jesus out to his followers saying, "Behold, the Lamb of God." Andrew, who immediately followed after Jesus, found his brother Simon Peter and said, "We have found the Messiah" (v. 41). The liturgy, like John the Baptist, points to Jesus and says to us, "Behold, the Lamb of God." Like Andrew, we are called to respond to the proclamation, to follow after Jesus, and with certainty to affirm, "I have found the Messiah." Without this response, our spiritual journey into Jesus cannot begin.

Once the spiritual journey into Jesus has begun, Jesus expects everything of us. James and John were in the boat mending nets with their father, Zebedee, when Jesus called them. Matthew tells us, "Immediately they left the boat and their father, and followed him" (Matt. 4:22). Discipleship requires an immediate and abrupt change of life. The early disciples underwent a radical reorientation of their allegiances, their occupations, their entire lives. An epiphany had occurred for them.

When they were addressed by Jesus they knew on the inside that this was it, this was what they had longed for, this was the fulfillment of their search. Today the liturgy proclaims Christ's claim over our lives and calls us into this kind of discipleship.

Christian discipleship cannot be reduced to a mere intellectual acquiescence. It demands more than lip service, more than attendance at worship and the functions of the church. It is a call to action. For as Jesus said to his disciples, "If any man would come after me, let him deny himself and take up his cross and follow me. For whoever would save his life will lose it, and whoever loses his life for my sake will find it" (Matt. 16:24–25). Spirituality is Christ living his life *in* us and *through* us. The manifestation of the glory of God made present in Jesus is to continue in his followers. Thus Jesus had to gather disciples in the first century even as he must in the twenty-first century. Therefore, we stand in line with the apostolic community, called of God as they were. Like them, we are called to drop the nets that occupy our lives and make Christ the first priority. But what does it mean to put Christ first, to follow him in radical obedience? The Gospel writers clarify this dimension of our spirituality as they lead us into the teaching of Jesus, an epiphany of his rule for our lives.

Training the Disciples

It is not enough for Jesus to say, "Come and follow me." After the disciples responded to the call to be a continuing epiphany of God's glory manifested in Jesus and in them, it was necessary for them to undergo a time of discipleship training. The Gospel writers, especially Matthew and Luke, move their readers from the call to discipleship to the training by Jesus in the Sermon on the Mount, a sermon that the liturgy after Epiphany wisely calls us to follow in our own spirituality.

First, in the Beatitudes (Matt. 5:1–12) Jesus teaches his disciples and us to turn the common vision of the world upside down. The common vision is that it is better to be aggressive than meek, better to be in charge than to be persecuted. But Jesus' teaching is that the poor, the oppressed, the downtrodden, the weak, and the persecuted have a special place in Jesus' heart because they know what it means to suffer. Because the gospel is not on the side of the wealthy and the powerful but the weak and lowly, Jesus, in this charter of Christian living, calls on his disciples to be meek, merciful, and pure in heart and to become peacemakers. Here for our time is a revolutionary epiphany that many Christians struggle to interpret, particularly those of us in the Western world, whose people consume more of the world's goods than any other people and where people live in countries in which power and prestige are more important than voluntary servanthood. Thus Jesus asks us as we embark on an Epiphany spirituality to examine our values, to refrain from ostentatious living, to look at life from the underside, to reach out and help the poor and oppressed by being on their side.

Next, Jesus teaches his disciples that by choosing poverty they will become the salt and light of the world (Matt. 5:13–16). His disciples are to be an epiphany of the glory of God to lead people out of an enslavement to the dark forces of life, to be a light to enlighten the whole world, and to call the world back into fellowship with its Creator and Lord. So Jesus' disciples are "salt of the earth" and "light of the world" (Matt. 5:13–14). The calling of the disciples and our calling today is to be transformed by the values of the kingdom so that we may draw others into the light. Jesus instructs his disciples to "let your light so shine before men, that they may see your good works and give glory to your Father who is in heaven" (Matt. 5:16).

Third, the fundamental approach to life to be taken by the disciples of Jesus is to live by the law of love. This love is what motivated God to send Jesus to fulfill the law of God's demands and to die to release us from the power of evil and enable us to choose the good. Consequently Jesus can call on his disciples and on us to "be perfect, as your heavenly Father is perfect" (Matt. 5:48). Jesus, by his life and death, has enabled us to reach for this perfection because he has conquered sin and revealed God's unconditional love. Therefore he can call his disciples to a radically new lifestyle by saying, "You have heard that it was said . . . but I say to you." Today the Epiphany liturgy calls us to turn away from the inverted values people live by, the lure of today's "you have heard that it was said" to the new values of Jesus that come from his "but I say to you." Jesus calls us to turn our backs on the dominance of whites over blacks, men over women, parents over children, and employer over employee. Instead we are to live by the law Jesus taught, namely to put ourselves in the shoes of the other person. This law extends even to our enemies, to those who persecute us and seek ill for our lives. God calls us to this kind of epiphany today, an epiphany of love characterized in our time by those who call us to love our neighbors, to serve their needs, and to build bridges toward peace.

Finally, this kind of love is one that serves the kingdom in a single passion—a passion that seeks to fulfill the injunction of Jesus to "seek first his kingdom and his righteousness" (Matt. 6:33). This kind of single-mindedness calls for a detachment from the things of this world that frequently demand a dedicated passion. Thus Jesus warns against a number of temptations, including the temptation to serve money (Matt. 6:19–21) and the temptation to be so concerned about the future that one's life is run by anxiety (Matt. 6:25–34). In addition, Jesus warns us against the appearance of serving God when the heart is elsewhere (Matt. 6:16–18). Serving God with single-mindedness does not mean Christians cannot marry, beget children, or have a vocation. It simply means the service of God in every area of life is of such a quality that one seeks to serve God in marriage or singleness, in work or pleasure, in life and death. In this way Jesus' disciples are not merely an epiphany of God's glory here or there or now and then, but they are a manifestation of God's love in Jesus continued in their lives in everything they say and do. The whole of life is so caught up in the service of the Master that no area of public or private life is divorced from the service of Christ.

We are the disciples whom Christ has called in the twenty-first century. The spirituality of love and service of God as the single passion of our lives is as viable today as in the first century. We are called to turn away from self-love and self-service, to abandon a life lived for self-gratification or self-glory, and to serve God as an epiphany of the self-giving service of Jesus. True spirituality longs for, seeks for, and wills this abandonment of self so that Christ may become present through our work, our lives, and our relationships, manifesting his power.

Epiphany calls for us to do more than follow after Jesus, learn of him, and be transformed by him. A number of Scripture readings such as the casting out of the unclean spirit (Mark 1:21–28), the healing of Peter's mother-in-law (Mark 1:29–31), the cleansing of the leper (Mark 1:40–45), and the healing of the paralytic (Mark 2:1–12) point to this dramatic aspect of Jesus' ministry. The meaning of these events is not isolated from the purpose of Jesus' mission to the world. He came to destroy the power of evil, to expunge Satan's debilitating effect on both the physical and spiritual side of human persons and the natural creation. These accounts are intended to lead us into an experience of Christ's transforming power over the evil effects of sin—a power that can touch our lives and heal us today.

Mark wants us to see both the power of evil to distort God's good creation and the greater power of Jesus to restore God's creation to wholeness. Like the characters in these Epiphany stories, we also experience physical, emotional, and spiritual scars that prevent us from the fullness of life God intends for us. All of us carry scars inflicted on us from the hardships of life. For some it may be a mental handicap that prevents us from grasping knowledge or skills that would fulfill our lives or enhance our expertise in work. For others a physical condition may stand in the way of doing simple things such as working, hearing, seeing, smelling, tasting, or telling. Perhaps we suffer from an emotional scar such as the loss of a parent or a child, or we have been abused or suffered the disorientation of divorce. All of these problems and more are addressed by Mark in these stories and show us that the issue of life that hurts us most is not beyond the healing and transforming power of Christ.

Recently on an outing to a Michigan beach I witnessed an eighteen-year-old boy in excellent physical condition do a flip into the water—a flip that resulted in a broken neck and instant paralysis. Although he was a stranger to me and others in our outing, our hearts were crushed for him and his family. Epiphany is a manifestation that his condition and the condition of all of us who suffer any kind of impairment is not ultimate. Although only relatively few people suffer physical or emotional conditions that bring life to a near halt, all of us do suffer in one way or another with conditions from which we wish to be free.

These Epiphany accounts give us a brief insight into the shalom of God that will eventually cover the earth. For Christ, by his death and resurrection, has come to destroy the powers of evil that distort human personality, disfigure the human body, pervert the mind, and crush the human spirit. There is no evil power, no sinister working that can stand before the empty tomb and survive, because Christ has already overcome all the forces of evil that marshal themselves against his created order. He will, as these accounts assure us, deliver us from any and all bondage and restore us to wholeness.

Epiphany also celebrates the transformation of the entire creation. God has come in Christ not only to restore the people he made but to renew the entire created order, to set it free from its "bondage to decay" (Rom. 8:21). Ancient Christianity in particular celebrates the forthcoming restoration of creation in its Epiphany liturgy. The following blessing of Epiphany, used in the ancient church, declares the human person is no longer the slave of cosmic forces: "Great art thou, Lord, and wonderful are thy works, and no word doeth justice to the praise of my wonders. . . . Before thee tremble supersensual powers; thee the sun praises, the moon worshippeth, the stars submit to thee, the light obeyeth, the tempest tremble, the springs worship thee. . . . Master thou couldest not bear to see mankind defeated by Satan, but didst come and save us. . . . Therefore, all creation hath praised thee in thine appearance."[4]

The Transfiguration

Although the calendar day of the transfiguration is August 6, the church wisely recalls the transfiguration on the last Sunday of Epiphany, which is the Sunday before Ash Wednesday and the beginning of our Lenten journey (see Mark 9:2–9; Luke 9:28–36).

We have already been given a hint to the future transfiguration of the world in the Epiphany readings. But here, in the transfiguration, we gain an intense manifestation of the future glory that will be revealed. The church fathers, especially the Greek fathers, made much of the transfiguration, for in it they saw not only the glory of God's essence shining forth in Jesus, but the essence of an Epiphany spirituality, the transformation of our own being by the presence of God.

An Epiphany Spirituality for Today

There are two sides to an Epiphany spirituality: Christ manifest *in* us, and Christ manifest *through* us. The early church fathers interpret the glory of God manifested as the dazzling light to Peter, James, and John as the true vision of the presence of the Divine in Christ, a presence made available to us through the power of the Holy Spirit. There is, of course, a qualitative difference between God present in Jesus and Jesus present in us. Jesus is God incarnate, the one man who participates in the actual essence of God. Thus, Paul tells us, "in him all the fullness of God was pleased to dwell" (Col. 1:19). But Christ *in* us is accomplished by the Holy Spirit, who urges us into conformity to the image of God perfectly expressed in Jesus. Through the Holy Spirit we are able to enter into a spiritual union with Christ, a union that effects a moral, intellectual, and social conformity to Christ, the model of true humanity. In this sense Christ is manifested in us, in our very being, in our personality, and in the values we choose.

Christ Manifest in Us

According to the early church fathers, a decisive way to unite with Jesus is through prayer. While there are many different kinds of prayer, the form of prayer advocated by the fathers to establish union with God is the short form. The short form is a brief prayer drawn from Scripture that is repeated over and over again. The most popular of the short form prayers is the Jesus Prayer, a lengthened version of the prayer said by the publican, "Lord Jesus Christ, Son of God, have mercy upon me a sinner" (see Luke 18:13). I have already mentioned this prayer as a spiritual discipline to be used at Christmas for Christ to be born within. It bears repeating as an Epiphany discipline for Christ born within to be continuously manifested within.

The purpose of the Jesus Prayer is to bring a person into union with Christ by fulfilling the mandate of Paul to "pray without ceasing" (1 Thess. 5:17 NRSV). Although it is a verbal prayer, the goal is for it to become a mental and spiritual prayer that is constantly in the mind and heart, a prayer that establishes a spiritual union with God through Christ.

An entire spiritual tradition known as the *Hesychast* method of prayer developed around the Jesus Prayer. In *The Way of the Pilgrim*, a spiritual classic on the Jesus Prayer, the prayer is described as follows:

The continuous interior prayer of Jesus is a constant uninterrupted calling upon the divine name of Jesus with the lips, in the spirit and in the heart; while forming a mental picture of His constant presence, and imploring His grace during every occupation, at all times, in all places, even during sleep. The appeal is couched in these terms, "Lord Jesus Christ, have mercy on me." One who accustoms himself to this appeal experiences, as a result, so deep a consolation and so great a need to offer the prayer always, that he can no longer live without it, and it will continue to voice itself within him of its own accord.[5]

I recommend Epiphany as a time to enter into an experience of constant union with Christ through the Jesus Prayer. I have listed below some of the rules for using this prayer suggested by the authors of the spiritual classic, *Unseen Warfare*, for those who are beginners with the Jesus Prayer:

1. Begin and end your current practice of prayer with the Jesus Prayer.
2. Increase the number of repetitions gradually as your enjoyment of the prayer grows.
3. Recite the prayer slowly and recite it as though you were standing before the Lord himself.
4. Repeat the prayer whenever you have free time, doing so in the intervals of your occupation and even in your talking.
5. Make certain the prayer comes from the heart and not merely from the lips.
6. Always act in a state of complete simplicity and great humility, never attributing success to yourself.
7. Do not set a time for achievement in this prayer. Decide only one thing: to work and to work. Months and years will go by before the first feeble indications of success begin to show.[6]

Make union with Christ a sincere goal of your Epiphany spirituality and realize that unless you are in union with Christ in your soul, you cannot manifest Christ in your life. I can attest to the value of the Jesus Prayer, as I find myself frequently saying it as I wait to sleep, as I walk or drive, as I face temptation, or as I find free time in my schedule here and there.

Christ Manifest through Us

An Epiphany spirituality is not only Christ in us but Christ being revealed *through* us to others. As God was manifested in Jesus Christ, so Christ is manifested through the church to the world. Because we are the church, the body of Christ who act as salt and light, we are the continuing manifestation of Christ's love and redeeming power.

Of course there are many ways we can express an Epiphany spirituality. For example, Christ is manifested in us when we live by the fruits of the Holy Spirit—love, joy, peace, patience, kindness, goodness, faithfulness, gentleness, and self-control. In the early church the fathers saw these fruits of the Spirit expressed in the gift of hospitality. Hospitality is a very special gift because it is a unique means through which Christ can be manifested. Therefore, the early church fathers had much to say about this gift and commended it as a special way to communicate the presence of Jesus.

The fathers ask us to consider how frequently God's presence is associated with hospitality in the Scripture. A special case in point is the hospitality Abraham offered to three men who appeared at the door of his tent (Gen. 18:1–15). In Christian iconography this event is interpreted as the visitation of the Triune God and has inspired the most famous of all icons, the icon of the Holy Trinity by Andrei Rublev. Abraham's hospitality to the three strangers is an inspiring example of the mutual exchange of God's presence that can occur in the gift of hospitality. While Abraham was manifesting the love of God to these men, they in turn manifested God's presence to Abraham and Sarah.

In keeping with the theme of Epiphany, the time in which Christ is manifested to the whole world, the liturgy of the church calls us to manifest Christ through hospitality. Hospitality evangelism is the kind of manifestation that may draw a stranger to the gospel into the very heart of Christ. Our world is full of lonely people—students, singles, the disabled, newcomers to town, the shy, the divorced, the aged, and the infirm. Like Abraham and Sarah we need to open up our homes and our lives to them, a hospitality that speaks volumes to the love and warmth of God.

Hospitality spirituality stands in the Western tradition of Christian spirituality. In the East, spirituality emphasizes solitude, being alone with the self as a way of practicing the presence of Jesus. But in the West, especially in modern times, there has been a great emphasis on a spirituality that reaches outward towards other people. While both spiritualities are needed for a well-rounded spirituality, Epiphany calls us to move outward toward others to bring them into the life of Christ in the Christian community.

All of us know one or more persons or families who live this way as a general rule. For example, I know of a university professor who purposely located himself at a university with many international students in order to have a hospitality ministry among them. The work of Francis Schaeffer at L'Abri, Switzerland, a ministry to students through his home, reached thousands of people. Covenant House, a ministry to prostitutes, drug addicts, and runaway children in New York, has touched thousands of lives through a hospitality spirituality. While these are well-known examples, the commitment to reach out to one person or one family is no less valuable in God's eye.

I recommend that you make this Epiphany special by choosing a person, a family, or a group of people to host and reach with the Good News. Use the Epiphany season to put into motion a lifelong commitment to reach out. There are a number of ways you can fulfill this calling: Establish a friendship with a stranger; invite a lonely person or family to dinner; begin a neighborhood Bible study and fellowship group in your home.

Conclusion

We gain insight into how Epiphany orders our spiritual lives by looking at the spiritual emphasis associated with Epiphany. It is clearly as the word itself means—a time for the manifestation of Jesus as the Christ, the fulfillment of all Israel's longing, and the fulfillment of the world's longing for a Savior. The three great events of the visit of the wise ones, the baptism of Jesus, and the marriage feast at Cana of Galilee express the manifestation of Jesus as the one who accomplishes God's mission.

Because God's glory has been manifested in Jesus Christ, he calls his disciples and us to manifest his glory by becoming his deeply committed disciples showing forth Christ through our lives. Consequently, for us an Epiphany spirituality is to allow Christ to be manifested in us through prayer and hospitality. May we open our hearts to God's epiphany within and may we reach out to be God's epiphany to the strangers in our midst.

Table 5: A Summary of Epiphany Spirituality

Theme	Spiritual Emphasis
What does Epiphany celebrate?	It manifests Jesus as the Son of God and Savior not only of Israel but of the whole world.
What is the focus of Epiphany day worship?	The coming of the three wise men to worship Jesus.
What is Epiphany spirituality?	That Christ may be manifested in us and through us.
What two incidents in the early ministry of Jesus especially manifest his mission?	The baptism of Jesus proclaims Jesus as God's Son, the Lamb of God who removes sin, the anointed one. The wedding feast reveals the glory of God in the paschal mystery.

Continued

What is the theme of all Sunday worship in the after Epiphany season?	The theme of all the Sundays in the after Epiphany season is the glory of God manifest in his Son.
What Epiphany events celebrate the manifest glory of God?	The calling of the disciples The training of the disciples The transfiguration of Jesus
How do we experience the manifest glory of God *in* us?	In *union* with Christ we are to be like him. Epiphany spirituality chooses, by the Spirit, to do what Jesus would do.
How is Christ *in us* achieved?	Through continuous prayer
How do we manifest Christ *through* us?	The fathers of the church identify hospitality as a primary context through which we manifest Christ.

A PRAYER FOR EPIPHANY

Give us grace, O Lord, to answer readily the call of our Savior Jesus Christ and proclaim to all people the good news of his salvation, that we and the whole world may perceive the glory of his marvelous works; who lives and reigns with you and the Holy Spirit, one God, forever and ever. Amen.

From *The Book of Common Prayer*

Questions for Reflection

1. What three or four insights have you gained about Epiphany spirituality?
2. How do the calling of the disciples, the training of the disciples, and the transfiguration speak to you of your own Epiphany spirituality?
3. To whom can you extend hospitality and manifest Christ?

Resources for the Day of Epiphany Worship and Preaching

See Robert Webber, ed., *The Services of the Christian Year*, vol. 5 of *The Complete Library of Christian Worship* (Peabody, MA: Hendrickson, 1994), 157–206.

- Introduction to Epiphany worship
- Resources for planning Epiphany worship
- The arts for Epiphany worship
- Sample services for Epiphany worship

TWO

THE CYCLE
OF LIFE

We now enter into the second cycle of Christian-year spirituality, the cycle of life. This cycle extends through Lent, Holy Week, and Easter, ending on Pentecost Sunday. In the cycle of life our spiritual journey changes significantly from the cycle of light. The emphasis of the cycle of light is on the incarnation, whereas the central motif of the cycle of life is the death and resurrection. However, there is fundamental unity between these cycles. Both have to do with the paschal mystery and the salvation of the world. One dwells on the incarnation while the other enters into the death and resurrection. One accents God coming among us in the person of Jesus of Nazareth; the other recalls the purpose for which he came—the self-giving sacrifice of his life to free the world from the domain of Satan and thus secure forgiveness and healing for the peoples of the world. Consequently, as we reflect on both the cycles of light and life, we are drawn into the inescapable fact of how the birth and death of Jesus are of a single piece, a garment that cannot be rent in two without doing violence to the Christian message.

There is also another way the cycles of light and life are brought together: both follow the pattern of expectation, fulfillment, and proclamation. Advent is expectation, Christmas is fulfillment, and Epiphany is proclamation; Lent is expectation, Easter is fulfillment, and Pentecost is proclamation. Thus there is a historical *progression* into both Christmas and Easter as well as spiritual *procession* from each. When we recall and relive the experience of God's people who pilgrimage into and out of the incarnation or into and out of the death and resurrection, we mark our own spirituality with expectation and fulfillment.

While the focus of our spirituality changes from the cycle of light to the cycle of life, the pattern of expectation, fulfillment, and proclamation remains the same.

The cycle of life was understood in great depth by the early church fathers centuries ago. The development of Lent, discussed in chapter 5, has one single purpose—to lead us into the very heart of the paschal mystery, the death and resurrection of Christ. The fathers of the church, standing in the tradition of the apostles, wanted to develop a spiritual exercise that would bring us into an experience of the death of death, the annihilation of hell, and the beginning of a new life. Lent is a journey into death, a death that will result in a new birth, a spiritual beginning again, for during Lent we journey into an event that not only happened in history as an actual occurrence that changed history but an event that happens within us. Christ conquered death, turning our death to sin into a resurrection to the fullness of life in the Spirit, which is available to us through faith. But this new life is not a mere proposition or a thing out there to be observed, analyzed, and systematized; it is to be experienced. It is a real, life-changing experience that shapes our vision of reality, informs our relationships, forms our values, puts us in touch with transcendence, and causes us to experience the spiritual dimension of life itself.

The very heart and source of the cycle of life climaxes in the three great days. In the early church Lent ended not on Palm Sunday but on Thursday of Holy Week. Thursday night, which in the Hebrew way of reckoning time is the beginning of Good Friday, is the starting time for the three great days in which the salvation of creatures and creation was accomplished. Chapter 6 traces those final events in the life of Christ and carries us into an experience of his final moments with his disciples, arrest, crucifixion, death, descent into hell, and glorious resurrection. In these events lie the deepest content and form of our spirituality, and his death and resurrection shape the pattern of our spirituality, which is to die to sin and be resurrected continuously to the life of the Spirit.

Chapter 7 presents the Easter season, which carries us into the true spiritual meaning of the physical resurrection of Jesus. During the seven weeks of the Easter season we are called by God to learn and relearn a resurrection spirituality, for Christ who died and is now raised is united to us and we to him in the very pattern of daily living. Signs of his omnipresence are given to us in the church through baptism and Eucharist. In and through the church and by the power of the Spirit special signs signify the presence of Jesus with us and we in him. These signs empower and free us to live in a resurrection spirituality. During Easter we also celebrate Ascension Day and the exalted reign of Christ over all creation. The Easter season ends with the day of Pentecost, which also marks the season known as "after Pentecost."

Chapter 8 deals with this time after Pentecost, which is also known as ordinary time. As I will show, even though it is called *ordinary time*, it is time that is *not* so ordinary because the emphasis is on Sunday worship that remembers God's entire action of salvation, anticipating that he who has been involved in history for our salvation brings history to its consummation. As the last Sunday of ordinary time demonstrates, Christ is King who rules over all.

The book concludes with a brief epilogue in which I encourage you to embrace the rhythm of Christian time as a way of ordering your spiritual life.

5

LENT

A Time to Repent

Although we praise our common Lord for all kinds of reasons, we praise and glorify him above all for the cross. [Paul] passes over everything else that Christ did for our advantage and consolation and dwells incessantly on the cross. The proof of God's love for us, he says, is that *Christ died for us while we were yet sinners.* Then in the following sentence he gives us the highest ground for hope: *If, when we were alienated from God, we were reconciled to him by the death of his Son, how much more, now that we are reconciled, shall we be saved by his life!*

John Chrysostom (AD 347–407)

Unfortunately some Christians live as though the death and resurrection of Jesus Christ never happened. Our lives become absorbed in the day-to-day experiences of life. We focus on name-brand clothing, the color of our houses, the size of our bank account, the year and make of our automobile, the prestige in which others hold us, and the symbols of our own power. We too easily forget our Maker and Redeemer, replacing God with things and ambition. Lent is the season that does something about this situation. It calls us back to God, back to basics, back to the spiritual realities of life. It calls on us to put to death the sin and the indifference we have in our hearts toward God and our fellow persons. And it beckons us to enter once again into the joy of the Lord—the joy of a new life born out of a death to the old life. This is what Ash Wednesday is all about—the fundamental change of life required of those who would die with Jesus and be raised to a new life in him.

Lent Begins with Ash Wednesday

For most people coming from my background, an Ash Wednesday service and Lent are quite foreign and somewhat threatening. The Christmas cycle is much less threatening because Christmas themes are so prevalent within our culture. Also, because the secularization of Christmas is so apparent, most Christians are attracted to the possibility of rising above the materialism of the Christmas culture. Consequently many Protestant churches now practice Advent, and more and more churches are open to Epiphany. But Lent is another matter. Lent appears to be dark and foreboding. It reminds Protestants of the Roman Catholic practices—ritualism, works, fasting, vigils, and the like. Haven't we been saved from all of that? Didn't the Reformers free us from having to do works and pilgrimages and such things?

No one would question that some Catholics have abused the real meaning of Ash Wednesday and Lent. We all remember those Catholic teenagers in high school; some of them may have been very poor representatives of the Catholic faith, but on Ash Wednesday they appeared with a dark smudge picturing the sign of the cross on their foreheads.

Perhaps we laughed inside and thought to ourselves, just another mark of an external, ritualistic religion. Perhaps yes, perhaps no. Only God can judge the heart. Aside from that dare we ask: Does something lie behind that symbol that has the potential to make our journey into Easter more meaningful? After all, what do we do for Easter? Most Protestants don't make any spiritual preparation for the annual celebration of the death and resurrection. For example, when I was growing up the only preparation for Easter made in my home—a deeply committed Christian home at that—was the planning and purchasing of new clothing. Easter was a weekend event. Preparing for Easter for seven weeks was unthinkable, ludicrous, even pagan. But now I am constrained to ask: Who is the pagan? Yes, it is wrong to go through the motions of Ash Wednesday and Lent in a mechanical, uninvolved way. But it is also wrong to ignore any kind of preparation for the Easter event. Happily there is an alternative for both Catholics and Protestants: *Recover the true spiritual intent of Ash Wednesday and the Lenten spiritual pilgrimage.* We can begin the journey into the spiritual meaning of Lent by looking at the life-changing content of the Ash Wednesday service.

Ash Wednesday

I will never forget the first Ash Wednesday service I attended. When I walked into the sanctuary I noticed how the decorum and mood of the people were so entirely different from that of the Christmas cycle. This mood immediately communicated the different nature of the spiritual discipline ordered by the Lenten season. The lights were dimmed, those already in the pews were quietly praying, as other people arrived they were greeted with quiet whispers, a simple nodding of the head, or silence. There seemed to be a seriousness attached to the worship into which we were entering, a somber spirit to which I was unaccustomed. I took my seat, and in the quietness of the moment, a silence not broken by organ music or friendly chatter, I bowed my head and waited for the service to begin.

There was no procession, no choir, no organ music. The celebrant, dressed in a black robe, simply walked out from a side door in the front and said in a hushed tone, "Let us pray." Then he slowly and deliberately prayed: "Almighty and everlasting God, you hate nothing you have made and forgive the sins of all who are penitent: create and make in us new and contrite hearts, that we, worthily lamenting our sins and acknowledging our wretchedness, may obtain of you, the God of all mercy, perfect remission and forgiveness; through Jesus Christ our Lord, who lives and reigns with you and the Holy Spirit, one God, forever and ever. Amen."[1]

Even as he prayed I sensed what was to become my Lenten spirituality: "Create and make in us new and contrite hearts." This pattern of repentance and conversion that was reiterated again in the service and expressed again and again throughout the season was calling me into a new and fresh experience with the healing reality of Jesus Christ.

I listened intently to the reading of the Scriptures that followed the prayer. The readings were Joel 2:1–2, 12–17; Psalm 103; 2 Corinthians 5:20–6:10; and Matthew 6:1–6, 16–21. While all these Scriptures speak to the pattern of renewal, calling us to repentance and conversion, the Gospel reading appears to set forth a blueprint for a Lenten spirituality. It calls us back to the basics, to God's love for us, and to our response to that love. In the Gospel reading appointed for Ash Wednesday, Jesus calls us to practice our piety in faith, to pray, to give alms, and to fast (Matt. 6:1–6, 16–21).

The emphasis is not faith as a mere belief system—an objective set of propositions to which we give intellectual assent—but faith as an embodiment, a life lived out in true piety characterized by prayer, almsgiving, and fasting. What lies at the root of each of these three practices of spirituality is not a mere rote, impersonal ritual but a truly engaging, demanding, and committed *relationship*.

The sermon that followed clarified how important it was for us to see fasting, prayer, and almsgiving in the perspective of faith. In the Gospel reading (Matt. 6:1–6, 16–21) and elsewhere Jesus chastises the Pharisees for improper motivation in the practice of fasting, prayer, and almsgiving. They do it to "be seen by men" (v. 5). They do not practice their piety in faith. The true evangelical reason we are called upon to fast, pray, and give alms is not so others will praise us but to establish, maintain, repair, and transform our relationship with God. When the Lenten discipline is not seen in terms of works or as a means of attaining God's favor but as a relationship with God, neighbor, and self, the discipline itself moves us to a deeper spirituality.

The Imposition of Ashes

The second part of the service is the imposition of ashes on the forehead. Like others in the service, my mood was one of deep quietness. I sat with head bowed meditating on my own sinfulness and my alienation from God, self, and neighbor. There flashed before me the faces of broken relationships, the remembrance of sins committed, and the sense of participating with the rest of the human race in a grand rebellion against God and God's will for the human family. I felt that my own Christian walk was characterized by some phoniness and desire to "be seen by others." As I was being moved to repentance, the celebrant began to read the call to the observance of a holy Lent:

> Dear People of God: the first Christians observed with great devotion the days of our Lord's passion and resurrection, and it became the custom of the Church to prepare for them by a season of penitence and fasting. This season of Lent provided a time in which converts to the faith were prepared for Holy Baptism. It was also a time when those who, because of notorious sins, had been separated from the body of the faithful were reconciled by penitence and forgiveness, and restored to the fellowship of the church. Thereby, the whole congregation was put in mind of the message of pardon and absolution set forth in the Gospel of our Savior, and of the need which all Christians continually have to renew their repentance and faith.
>
> I invite you therefore, in the name of the Church, to the observance of a holy Lent, by self-examination and repentance; by prayer, fasting and self-denial; and by reading and meditating in God's holy Word. And, to make a right beginning of repentance and as a mark of our mortal nature, let us now kneel before the Lord, our maker and redeemer.[2]

I knelt in silence for several minutes, savoring the words that invited us to the observance of a holy Lent. My mind drifted from thoughts about my own pilgrimage to thoughts about the reason we are called to the practice of Lent—the passion of the Lord Jesus Christ. I knew that what I wanted was a true and real entrance into the passion of Christ. I wanted to die with Christ and be buried with him so I could be raised in the resurrection to the newness of life. I then heard the words of the celebrant, "I invite those who wish to come and identify with Christ through the imposition of ashes, to proceed forward." I stood to my feet and with many others walked silently to the altar rail and knelt, waiting for the ashes to be placed on my forehead. I listened intently as the celebrant prayed: "Almighty God, you have created us out of the dust of the earth: grant that these ashes may be to us a sign of our mortality and penitence, that we may remember that it is only by your gracious gift that we are given everlasting life; through Jesus Christ our Savior. Amen."[3]

As I knelt with my head slightly tilted upward to receive the ashes of the burnt palm leaves from Palm Sunday of the year before, I let the words "a sign of our mortality" burn into my heart. Like so many others, I live as though I will never die; it is not on my agenda of things to do. But in that moment I was reminded of my own mortality, the short duration of my own life, and of the accountability of my own life to God. Sobered by the reality of death, I tilted my head higher as the celebrant dipped his thumb into the ashes, and I allowed myself to feel the moisture of the ashes and the pressure of his thumb throughout my whole body as he made the sign of the cross on my forehead and intoned those chilling words, "Remember that you are dust, and to dust you shall return."

I returned to my seat and waited silently as others received the imposition of ashes. In the silence of those moments I listened to the continuous repetition of those words, "Remember that you are dust, and to dust you shall return," as I watched the people kneel, receive the imposition of ashes, and return to their seats. I love to watch people because they communicate so much through their faces. While these faces were sober, there was also a quiet peace present in their eyes and demeanor, a peace that went beyond the sobriety of the moment and spoke of the resurrection to come.

The Litany of Penitence

Gathered once again into silence, the celebrant led us in the reading of Psalm 51 in *The Book of Common Prayer*. I had read that psalm many times in my life and had even heard sermons on it, but it had never touched me in the depths of my being as it did that night. As I said, "Have mercy on me, O God, according to your loving kindness; in your great compassion blot out my offenses. Wash me through and through from my wickedness and cleanse me from my sin" (vv. 1–2), I sensed an overwhelming reality of the presence of God. I was not just saying words; God was there standing before me, as it were, listening to me pour out a reality that reached into my inner self and expressed what I felt in my gut. I cried with the psalmist, "Against you only have I sinned. . . . Purge me from my sin, and I shall be pure. . . . Hide your face from my sin" (vv. 4, 7, 9). And then with the psalmist I shifted into the position of pleading with God to "change me and make me new. . . . Create in me a clean heart, O God, and renew a right spirit within me; cast me not away from your presence and take not your holy spirit from me; give me the joy of your saving help again and sustain me with your bountiful spirit" (vv. 10–12). The sense that God would in fact do this for me so long as I came to him as a child in fullness of faith and trusting in him alone swept over me and touched my heart. Then I heard the concluding words of comfort, "The sacrifice of God is a troubled spirit; a broken and contrite heart, O God, you will not despise" (v. 17). Here, I thought, is *the* psalm for Lent, a psalm to return to again and again in my journey into the passion of Christ. Here is what God wants of me—a spirit that is truly broken of pride and self-sufficiency, a heart that feels its own willful path, a path that has led itself away from the presence of God and an obedience to his will for my life.

Like others, though, I need to have my sins spelled out clearly. I am so hardened to my own sinful condition that I tend to overlook my sin, even deny it or name it something other than sin. Fortunately the worship of the Ash Wednesday service did not leave me with only a generic sense of my condition, but following the praying of Psalm 51, the Litany of Penitence made me aware in a concrete and particular fashion of the extent of my sin. I found these prayers to be uncomfortable because they were telling the truth about me—truths I didn't want to admit. But I knew I had to face these truths if I was to experience a Lent that truly moved me to repentance and a newness of life in Christ.

The prayers spoke to me of the hardness of my own heart and the tendency of my life to be only superficially committed to Christ as the Lord of my entire life. The celebrant prayed, "We have not loved you with our whole heart and mind and strength. We have not loved our neighbors as ourselves. We have not forgiven others, as we have been forgiven."[4] I reluctantly agreed that this was true. I reflected on my own halfhearted service of God and my interest in serving self, even in ministry, and I was struck by the depth of this prayer. I knew I had something to work on here, a matter that could, if I let it, order my entire Lenten experience.

Then the prayers turned to the specific ways I and others turn away from God and serve the idols of self. "We confess to you, Lord, all our past unfaithfulness: the pride, hypocrisy and impatience of our lives, our self indulgent appetites and ways, our exploitation of other people, our anger at our own frustration, our envy of those more fortunate than ourselves, our intemperate love of worldly goods and comforts, our dishonesty in daily life and work, our negligence in prayer and worship and our failure to commend the faith that is in us."[5] Even though with others I kept saying, "We confess to you, Lord," I knew Lent was a call to go beyond the mere words of repentance and adopt an action that would see real change in my life in every one of these areas. It occurred to me that I could make a list of these sins of self and find one or more specific examples of each in my own life.

First, the image of sins against self were being portrayed in my own mind. Then the prayers shifted to sins against my neighbor. A whole new list began to emerge. "Accept our repentance, Lord, for the wrongs we have done: for our blindness to human need and suffering, and our indifference to injustice and cruelty, for all false judgments, for uncharitable thoughts toward our neighbors and for prejudice and contempt toward those who differ from us."[6] Like others who live in the privileged wealth, status, and freedom of middle-class America, I sense that I live and act as though I have the right to the good life. These prayers reached inside of me and touched me with the reminder that my good fortune is in a certain sense at the expense of another's loss—and my Lord's call to almsgiving as a special concern of the Lenten journey struck me with greater meaning.

Finally, the prayers turned to my sinful relationship with the creation, with nature itself. I heard the celebrant confessing for me as he quietly but forcefully prayed, "for our waste and pollution of your creation and our lack of concern for those who come after us."[7] I thought of the energy I consume and my lack of interest in the environmental issues that revolve around the raping of our created order and wreckage we will pass down to our children and children's children.

As I reflected on these prayers I was encountered in a new way by the extent of my alienation. I was reminded that as a sinner I am alienated from God, self, neighbor, and nature. Even as one who has confessed Christ to be Lord, as one who wants to follow after Christ, I am still involved in a sinful disobedience and indifference to all these areas of life. Lent, I reminded myself, is the time to take a good look at these sins, the time to fast from these sins, to enter into a deeper prayer relationship with God, the time to extend myself in compassionate love and caring to my neighbor and my world. Lent orders this kind of spirituality—a spirituality of repentance that leads to the cross and the tomb.

If the service had ended with the Litany of Penitence, I would have been devastated. I can only take so much of the dark side of life. The soul becomes quickly downcast and burdened by its sinfulness. It needs something more. Fortunately, the service did not end there. We passed the peace. As I said, "The Peace of the Lord be with you," shook hands with my neighbor, and heard the words, "Peace be with you," I was hearing the resurrection. Here in these words that Jesus first spoke to his disciples in the upper room (see Luke 24:36–49) is the promise that the dark side of life in the world and in us will not prevail. The power of the evil one has been overcome. There is light at the end of the tunnel. As the service ended with the Eucharist, we glimpsed the promise of the resurrection, a foretaste of the Easter event that lies beyond the cross and the tomb. But I knew for now the resurrection was a promise—a promise that would turn into a reality if I journeyed faithfully through the Lenten discipline. I sensed I must die with him if I am to be raised with him. This is what I wanted, an *experience* of the death and resurrection of Christ, not a mere cognitive assent to a fact that didn't touch me in the depth of my very being.

Lenten Themes

While the Ash Wednesday service marks out our spirituality for Lent, the worship of the following Sundays orders our spirituality in such a way that we are enabled to sustain the repentance to which we have been called.[8]

The Temptation of Christ

The first Sunday after Ash Wednesday asks us to mark our spirituality by the temptation of Christ (Matt. 4:1–11; Mark 1:9–13; Luke 4:1–13). In this reading we find Christ, who is tempted by the devil, overthrowing the power of the devil and avoiding the temptation of Satan to establish the kingdom in a way other than the cross.

The early church fathers loved to dwell on the comparison between the first Adam and Christ the second Adam, a comparison made by Paul in Romans 5:12–21 and 1 Corinthians 15:20–28. The first Adam did something *to* us. He brought sin, death, and condemnation and triggered the chain of events that brought ruin to the human family. But the second Adam did something *for* us. He reversed what the first Adam did, bringing life, righteousness, and justification and setting into motion a new chain of events that will eventually bring redemption to the whole world.

The church fathers saw the temptation as a turning point in the process of reversing the human situation. For here, the fathers tell us, is the exact counterpart to Adam. Adam yielded to the temptation. Christ overcame the temptation.

Christ not only overcame the temptation for himself, he overcame it for us. Orthodox Christianity has always taught the incarnation was not simply the vehicle for God to be with us but the reality of God becoming one of us and doing for us what we cannot do for ourselves. Because we are of the first Adam, we cannot overcome temptation by ourselves. Like Adam we face temptation and yield to it. But because Christ became one of us and was fully human in every respect, we can share in his conquering of the evil one.

The serpent in the Garden of Eden and the tempter in the wilderness represent the enticement to sin that lies in the very structure of the world itself. It appears here and there at work, in the home, and in our relationships. We express our service to the tempter through our selfishness, ambition, pride, lack of integrity, anger, lack of compassion, willingness to put other people down, and in many other ways.

Lent is a time to intentionally confront all the ways the first Adam continues to control our lives, to carry these ways to the cross, to let them be crucified with Jesus, and to bury them in the tomb never to rise again. Through this journey we enter into his death and become new creatures in the resurrection. For as Jesus overcame temptation for us, he delivered us from it in the resurrection.

The Scriptures present two pictures of the human person: the one as he or she is, the other as he or she ought to be. Through Christ God calls us to a newness that can begin when we allow Christ who overcame temptation to be the Christ who lives in us to confront the temptations that come our way. Lent is the time to will Christ's presence in our lives, to choose him as the model for our living, and to call upon him through the name of Jesus to be present at every temptation, to dispel the power of the evil one, and to set us free from the destructive power of evil.

The Call to Deny Sin

The second Sunday of Lent calls on us to deny the power of evil over our lives (Mark 8:31–38; Luke 13:22–35; John 3:1–17). The temptation to sin, to do what we know to be fundamentally wrong, to live a life oriented toward our own self-centeredness, sustains a powerful hold over our lives.

Nicodemus (John 3:1–17) is told to cease defining himself by the world of his own making. He is to deny his own present situation with such a decisive repudiation and to affirm Jesus with such a life-changing embrace that this change can be described as a new birth. Certainly Nicodemus, a Pharisee and ruler of the Jews, had all the trappings of a prosperous, successful, and deeply religious man. But Jesus knew what was on the inside of this man.

During Lent God may call us, as he called Nicodemus, to abandon the world of our pharisaic religion, to stop pretending we are righteous, to come to grips with the reality of our own phoniness, and to break through to a faith that is real and genuine. Like Nicodemus we need to cut through the shackles that bind us to the powers controlling our lives. We need to deny the powers that control us, turn our backs on them, and go in a new direction. Perhaps this new direction will come from the abandonment of a deep-seated habit that holds us in its grip. Perhaps there is a need to have a breakthrough in a relationship with a friend or with someone who is no longer a friend. Perhaps we need to forgive someone of a wrong done to us in the past. These are the kinds of sins that hold us back from the experience of a more complete newness. Once they are cared for, a rush of newness comes upon us because we have denied the power of sin over us and turned ourselves toward an obedience to Christ's will for our lives, which allows us to experience a freedom from sin that makes us feel we have a fresh start, a new birth.

The Call to Repentance

The third Sunday of Lent follows a progressive line from the first and second Sundays. It brings our spiritual experience from dealing with temptation, to a denial of the power of evil over our lives, through to the place of repentance. Here is a biblical process: face our sin; say no to sin; repent of sin. A striking example is the woman of Samaria (John 4:5–26). In this interesting and compelling story we are able to see several vivid truths concerning our own repentance. First, when Jesus asks the woman of Samaria to give him a drink, we gain an insight into God's basic attitude toward us: God wants something from us. God thirsts for something from us. God thirsts for us to turn away from sin through confession and repentance. God wants us to acknowledge our sins and to identify the nooks and crannies of our lives not turned over to the Spirit. In repentance we turn away from sin and determine with God's power to walk in newness of life.

The story of the woman at the well also shows us that God meets us where we are. From the human perspective the meeting between Jesus and the woman appears to be a happenstance. She went to the well to get water and Jesus just happened to be there. From a divine standpoint, though, we can see that no matter where we are or no matter where we go, Jesus is there to meet us and to touch us with his healing power. God is inescapably present in every facet of our lives. When we go shopping, to a movie, or to a business meeting, God is there. Our needs are met by God at any time and any place. God only asks that we meet Christ with an open heart and a willingness to bare all that God already knows and then to turn toward God in simple faith and trust.

The story of the encounter between Jesus and the woman at the well is a prime story for Lent. It was originally used among the catechumens who were preparing for baptism—a journey to be completed on Easter morning. It was powerful for them as it should be for us because it is a call back to the most basic and rudimentary truth of the gospel— repentance and transformation. In Lent we are called to once again experience the first love of faith, the breath of fresh air in the newness of our experience with Jesus. Lent is to stir up that original passion within us, to build a fire in the belly, to inspire within us the glow of first love. This can happen to us when we meditate on the story of the woman at the well, for she takes us to where we can meet Christ in the most basic and simple needs of our life experience.

Lent calls us to truly seek God, to look for God in every area of our lives, and to claim God's presence for our sake. A basic rule of the spiritual pilgrimage according to St. Benedict is, "Does he really seek God?" Lent calls us to a repentance that expresses itself in a seeking like the psalm sung by the ancient catechumens, "As a deer goes crazy looking for water in the desert, so I am going crazy looking for you my God" (Ps. 42:1, ancient translation).

Healing and Conversion

The fourth Sunday of Lent is known as Rose Sunday. It is a Sunday that strikes a more joyous note than previous Sundays of Lent because it shifts away from an emphasis on the repentance of the sinner to Christ's healing power. It is thought that the note of joy on this Sunday originates from the rite of the catechumens known as the "opening of the ears"—a ritual symbolizing the gift of hearing the Word of God and responding to it in faith. This represents a turning point from repentance to faith, a joyous occasion indeed. The wearing of rose-colored vestments on this Sunday, a sign of that joy, probably originated in the medieval era as a custom to welcome the coming of spring. This celebration symbolizes the joy of salvation, a welcome respite in the middle of a long season of repentance and preparation.

The readings for this Sunday order our spiritual pilgrimage into an experience of the healing power of Christ. He heals the man born blind (John 9:1–13). He discourses on the healing power of the bread of life (John 6:25–59) and tells the story of the prodigal who was healed and returned to his father (Luke 15:11–32). In each of these stories the accent is on what God can do for us when we repent and turn to the grace he offers. The story of the man born blind is especially instructive as a Lenten story. In the early church, baptism and conversion into the church was called an "enlightenment." It was viewed as the falling away of the scales of blindness, an entrance into a new vision of things.

The fourth Sunday of Lent is a joyous Sunday because it allows a momentary experience of the resurrection in an otherwise bleak, dreary, and somber spiritual pilgrimage. Many churches do something special after the service on this Sunday to mark the day with a bit of celebration and gaiety. A favorite is the cake walk. Many cakes are brought to the walk, but one special "Rose Cake" is to be won and taken home by the winner. The walk itself is a fun-filled event many of us have done at parties. A group marches around a set number of chairs to joyous music. There is always one less chair than people. When the music stops, the person left standing is out. Another chair is removed, and the march continues. The last one to sit gets the cake. Then the whole community joins in the "cake party." The joy and fun of it in the middle of Lent is a foretaste of the resurrection to come—a welcome stop at an oasis in the desert spirituality of Lent.

A Foretaste of Easter

The final Sunday before Palm Sunday and the beginning of Holy Week orders our spirituality toward the coming death and resurrection and call us into a more intense spiritual preparation for the paschal mystery (Luke 20:9–19; John 11:1–17; 12:20–33). In the ancient church this fifth Sunday of Lent was called the "First Sunday of the Passion." On this Sunday Christians veiled the cross and other objects in the church that symbolized Christ and his work on the cross. The veiling of the Christ symbols has been viewed differently by various commentators. Most agree that it is a way of communicating the humiliation of God in the voluntary death of Jesus, a symbol to impress upon us the steep cost God was willing to pay for our redemption.

The story of Lazarus (John 11:1–17) captures the spiritual experience of preparing for the great paschal mystery. The death of Lazarus is a symbol of our own dead spiritual condition. During Lent we are called on to look at our own deadness and to act on it. In this week we look at the juxtaposition of death and resurrection. We are called not to remain dead but to be raised to newness of life, to new birth, to a fresh and new encounter with Jesus. Some of us are spiritually dead because our faith is purely intellectual. We believe the right things. We adhere to the creeds, the confessions, and the doctrines of the church. But there is no *life* in us, we simply acquiesce to the tradition for tradition's sake. We believe that we believe, but we know that is not enough. Others of us are dead because we have a total lack of feeling. We are not moved by the worship of the church, by song and prayer, by Eucharist and festivity. It is there, but it isn't real, it doesn't touch us in the inner recesses of our being. And we feel cold, numb, and dead.

The God who raised Lazarus from the dead can raise us up from our intellectualized and nominal faith. As Jesus called forth life in Lazarus (John 11:38–44), so God can resurrect us to new life in the resurrection of Jesus. God, who raised Jesus from the dead, can raise us up to a new experience of spiritual life surging within us. The key is to unravel the rags of self-righteousness and to surgically remove the sin that stands in the way of God breaking in on us in refreshing new ways. This can only happen when we choose to take our sins and our indifference to the cross and the tomb and let them be buried there so we can rise with Christ, committed to serve him in a new and radically devout way. Our spiritual journey this week proceeding out of this consciousness prepares us to walk the road to Jerusalem and to enter into the final stages of death with our Lord during Holy Week. This is the way to experience redemption. We must know who we are and where we fall short of a true following after Jesus. Then we must take the specifics of our self-understanding to the grave so we may rise with Christ anew. This is how Lent orders our spirituality.

Lenten Spirituality

Throughout the preceding pages I have made reference here and there to the rite of baptism. From the earliest days of the church's experience of Lent, baptism has always been the center symbol of a Lenten spirituality along with fasting, prayer, and almsgiving.

The Lenten discipline originated with the catechumens who were preparing for baptism in the early church. As early as the *Didache*, a writing circulating among Christians possibly in the late first century, mention was made of preparing for baptism through a period of instruction and fasting. "Giving public instruction on all these points . . . before the baptism, moreover, the one who baptizes and the one being baptized must fast, and any others who can. And you must tell the one being baptized to fast for one or two days beforehand."[9] The "any others who can" meant the whole Christian community was to join the converting catechumens as they traveled toward their own baptism. Those already baptized adopted as their spiritual discipline a similar spiritual pilgrimage. Later the pilgrimage became forty days long and led to the reaffirmation of the baptismal vows of the entire community.

Baptismal Spirituality

The Lenten journey is a baptismal spirituality. It is rooted in repentance and conversion, the putting off of the old life and the putting on of the new. Contrary to the opinion of some, this movement from one condition to another is not necessarily a punctilious experience, although there is a point of beginning. Rather, it is a continuous action, a constant turning away from sin toward God throughout one's entire life. Lent is the primary season for this dynamic of baptismal spirituality. Lent orders our spirituality back to its beginnings, back to the basics of repentance and faith. Luther captured the meaning of Lenten spirituality when he called upon his followers to "live in your baptism." To live in one's baptism is to be continually renewed by the commitment of our original spiritual experience.

A glance at the baptismal vows reveals to us the powerful impact living in our baptism can make on spirituality. First, baptism into Christ is a calling to turn away from evil and to renounce its power in our lives. In the early church the renunciation of evil in the rite of baptism was a powerful experience of literally choosing to turn one's back on sin. The celebrant would ask, "Do you renounce the devil and all his works?" The one being baptized would turn to the west, the symbolic direction of the evil one, and say, "I renounce him and all his works," and would then spit, symbolically spitting in the face of Satan as a sign of ending that relationship. Today in baptism we may be asked:

Do you renounce Satan and all the spiritual forces of wickedness that rebel against God?

Do you renounce the evil powers of the world, which corrupt and destroy the creatures of God?

Do you renounce all sinful desires that draw you from the love of God?

This renunciation is the negative side of Lenten spirituality. The positive side of spirituality is to turn to Jesus, who by his death and resurrection has dethroned Satan and curtailed his power in our lives. When we turn to Jesus we claim his victory over the power of evil *for us*. We acknowledge that if Christ be for us none can be against us (Rom. 8:31). We turn from "the course of this world" (Eph. 2:2) and are "raised . . . up with him" (Eph. 2:6) in a newness of life. For example, in the ancient church the candidate for baptism was asked to express faith in Jesus Christ. Today the celebrant asks:

Do you turn to Jesus Christ and accept him as your Savior?
Do you put your whole trust in his grace and love?
Do you promise to follow and obey him as your Lord?[10]

Lenten spirituality asks us to review our vows and enter into a fresh conversion experience with Jesus Christ by an act of *metanoia* (turning), a turning from sin to Christ. To assist us in this pilgrimage Lent calls us to fast, pray, and give alms. The evangelical nature of these actions is to help us to actually embody what it means to turn from sin and put our trust in Jesus.

Fasting, Praying, Almsgiving

I have already mentioned the evangelical nature of fasting. The purpose of the fast with the accompanying prayer and resulting almsgiving is not to accumulate works and gain favor in the eyes of God. Such a view is unbiblical and leads to legalism. Rather, the purpose of fasting is to establish, maintain, repair, and transform our relationship with God. For fasting, prayer, and almsgiving are means through which we express our spiritual pilgrimage during Lent, and through these means we experience the turning away from sin and conversion to Christ ordered by the spirituality of Lent.

Fasting, prayer, and almsgiving is not only the act of giving up something such as food, time, and money. It is also the activity of taking something on. When we give up a sin that has its grip on our lives, we need to replace it with a positive alternative. Our Lenten spirituality not only calls on us to turn away from a sin that holds us in its power but to turn toward a virtue that replaces our sin.

For example, fasting from food is a symbol of the discipline it takes to turn away from our sin. Prayer is the actual experience of turning to God in dependence. Almsgiving is the symbol of the virtue we are taking on to replace our sin. Consequently, it is of utmost importance for us to do the actual act of fasting, prayer, and almsgiving *simultaneously* with the turning away from a sin and turning toward a virtue. The two actions interlock with each other in such a way that success in one discipline corresponds with our achievement in the other. If we fail to keep the discipline of fasting, prayer, and almsgiving, the chance of succeeding in overcoming our sin and transplanting it with a virtue are severely weakened.

Fasting does not stand by itself but must be integrated into a lifestyle emphasizing a relationship with God, self, and others. There is an internal and external rhythm to fasting and turning from sin. It includes the *inner purification* that comes from fasting and turning from sin. On the one hand there is a ridding oneself of the poisons and toxins that build up in the system and prevent the fullness of life. On the other hand there is a fresh start, a new beginning that expresses itself in the fulfillment of the purgation. And that fresh start is the accomplishment of a fresh relationship with God, with self, and with neighbor expressed in the tangible act of almsgiving and the adoption of a virtue to replace the purged sin.

There are two kinds of fasting adopted during Lent—the total fast and the ascetical fast. The total fast is for a short period of time—a day or even less. It is usually associated with a special day such as Ash Wednesday or the three great days (Triduum) from the Maundy Thursday evening liturgy to the Great Paschal Vigil of Easter. One does not do the fast simply to fast but to experience the spiritual rhythm of expectation and fulfillment. Here again the external discipline orders the internal experience. The expectation that comes from the denial of food in fasting is almost always connected with its movement toward participation in the Eucharist at the end of the day, which brings fulfillment to the expectation. Spiritually we focus our day around the bread of heaven and the cup of salvation. We learn to meditate on the meaning of bread and drink and the healing presence of Jesus at the table. We long to be with Christ, to be touched by him in our inner person, to be healed of our pain, and to be stimulated toward the fulfillment of the virtue we seek to adopt.

By contrast, the ascetical fast occurs over a longer period of time and concentrates on a disciplined diet. One may choose to drop meats or sweets or perhaps to eat only one meal a day during an ascetical fast. The purpose of this fast is to be liberated from the flesh. This fast controls the passion for food in order to deal with a passion of another sort that holds us in its grip. The purpose of the ascetical fast is to liberate us from the power that flesh holds over the spirit, the power that brought Adam into ruination. For example, a person may fast as a means to experience victory over jealousy, envy, anger, lust, lack of integrity, or some other such issue that has been identified as a problem area in his or her life.

In the ascetical fast the time factor is important. The power of evil at work in our lives is not usually overcome in a single experience.

Certainly we should not deny that possibility. There are cases in which God delivers one from alcohol, from drugs, from a wasted life, or even from something much less pronounced in a dramatic healing. But for most of us conversion is subtle and gradual rather than dramatic and instant. Also, God works in conjunction with our own will. Consequently, the ascetical fast that deals with an issue of character development requires choice and intention on our part. We have to exercise the power of our own will over against the powers of evil that continually draw us into habits of life that are contrary to the gospel. The demonic powers at work against us can only be overcome by fasting and prayer. Because Lent is the time to identify with the death of Christ, a death in which we participate through our conversion and baptism, it is also the time to identify a power working against us and crucify it with Christ and bury it in the tomb, never to be raised again.

Sunday is never a fast day because Sunday is the day of the resurrection, a day that transcends time and participates in the time that is to come. This future time is made present now in a practical way in the rest and anticipation of rejoicing and feasting, not a day of fasting.

A Suggested Discipline

A specific example of a Lenten discipline for us to adopt and practice is found in St. Ephrem the Syrian, a fourth-century spiritual writer. A Lenten prayer he wrote is to this day prayed in the Eastern Orthodox Church every evening from Monday through Friday during Lent. Here is the text:

> O Lord and Master of my life!
> Take from me the spirit of sloth, faint-heartedness, lust of power and idle talk.
> But give me rather the spirit of chastity, humility, patience and love to my servant.
> Yea, O Lord and King!
> Grant me to see my own errors and not to judge my brother; for thou art blessed unto ages of ages. Amen.[11]

Through this prayer we encounter four negative concerns aimed at spiritual struggles common to us all:

> Sloth—a laziness that prevents us from choosing a spiritual pilgrimage aimed at overcoming the powers of evil working against us.
> Faintheartedness—despondency, a negative and pessimistic attitude toward life.

Lust of power—the assertion of self as lord of life expressed in the desire to subordinate other people under our power.

Idle talk—a negative power of speech that puts others down and uses words in a destructive rather than constructive way.

These four negative characteristics deny us the fullness of life intended by God. They are balanced by four positive characteristics that bring us into greater experience with the fullness of life God intends for us:

Chastity/wholeness—the word is most often used regarding sexuality. But its real meaning is the opposite of sloth and refers to wholeness. Broadly speaking it refers to the recovery of true values in every area of life.

Humility—the fruit of wholeness is humility, the victory of God's truth taking hold in our entire life. The humble person lives by the truth of God and sees life as God has made it and intended it to be.

Patience—patience sees the depth of life in all its complexity and does not demand instant change now, in this moment.

Love—the opposite of pride. When wholeness, humility, and patience are worked in us, the result is a person characterized by love. This kind of person is one who can sincerely pray, "Grant me to see my own errors and not to judge my brother."

I suggest you memorize this prayer and repeat it frequently during the days of Lent. In the morning meditate on the four powers from which you seek to be delivered—sloth, faintheartedness, lust of power, and idle talk. At noon meditate on the four virtues you desire to experience in your life—chastity/wholeness, humility, patience, and love. During each day determine to find a specific situation in which you can exercise one or more of both the negative and positive disciplines. Then in the evening when you pray the prayer again, review the events of the day and identify the way in which you have fulfilled one or another of these spiritual goals. To be most effective this prayer and the form it takes in your life should be coupled with fasting from food (ascetical fast) and the giving of alms (preferably to the poor).

From Palm Sunday to Wednesday of Holy Week

We should not look on Palm Sunday simply as a day to recall the entry of Jesus into Jerusalem. It is that, but it is more. It is our own entry into the most solemn yet the most glorious experience of spirituality. For

Jesus, Palm Sunday was his gateway to the culminating events of his earthly life. As we enter that gate with him, our spiritual lives are being ordered into the most sacred moments of the history of the world and of our own experience with the meaning of human existence.

Palm Sunday

In the liturgical church Palm Sunday normally begins outside the church on the lawn before the front door. The gathering outside the church is a symbol of Christ together with his people outside the gate of Jerusalem getting ready for the week of all weeks. The first time I stood there with the crowd I sensed that what was to begin was a weeklong service of worship, broken in various parts to be sure, but a weeklong pilgrimage into a personal experience with Christ rejected, crucified, buried, and risen. I sensed the mystery of it all and waited with anticipation for the drama to begin.

The service began as the celebrant who was standing in the midst of us cried, "Blessed is the King who comes in the name of the Lord." As we responded with the words, "Peace in heaven and glory in the highest," I felt as though the original action of Palm Sunday was happening all over again. I was there with the crowd at the gate of Jerusalem greeting Jesus as he entered the city.

The celebrant then prayed a prayer that included the words, "Assist us mercifully . . . that we may enter with joy upon the contemplation of those mighty acts, whereby you have given us life and immortality."[12] The heart and mind flashed forward to the events of the week ahead, allowing me to momentarily sense the spiritual pilgrimage I was about to take into the heart of the most important events of human history.

My attention was brought back to my place at the gate of Jerusalem as a reader read in a loud, clear voice the account of Jesus entering the city (Matt. 21:1–11). As he came to those words, "And when he entered Jerusalem, all the city was stirred, saying 'Who is this?'" (v. 10), I sensed that even though I knew the answer to that question in my head, I was being called to answer it from the heart. At that moment I heard the minister cry, "Let us give thanks to the Lord our God," and with the crowd I responded, "It is right to give him thanks and praise." Then I followed intently the prayer that laid before me the meaning of our worship for that day:

> It is right to praise you, Almighty God, for the acts of love by which you have redeemed us through your Son Jesus Christ our Lord. On this day He entered the holy city of Jerusalem in triumph, and was proclaimed as King of kings by those who spread their garments and branches of palm

along His way. Let these branches be for us signs of victory, and grant that we who bear them in His name may ever hail Him as our King, and follow Him in the way that leads to eternal life; who lives and reigns in glory with you and the Holy Spirit, now and forever. Amen.[13]

As I was meditating on the words, "Let these branches be for us signs of victory," the celebrant cried, "Blessed is he who comes in the name of the Lord." Together with the crowd I responded, "Hosanna in the highest." Then in quick, successive action we turned to process into the church, receiving a palm in our hands as we joined voices to sing:

> All glory, laud and honor
> To Thee, Redeemer, King!
> To whom the lips of children
> Made sweet hosannas ring.[14]

As I took my seat I sensed I had entered into the gate of Jerusalem and stood with the crowd in the city. To this point every part of the service expressed the joy and excitement of the crowds who originally welcomed Jesus into Jerusalem. But the mood was soon to change. The crowds thought they were welcoming a king who would overthrow the Roman yoke and set up another kingdom like that of David. But they were soon to be disappointed, and many who had cried, "Hosanna to the Son of David! Blessed is he who comes in the name of the Lord! Hosanna in the highest!" (Matt. 21:9), were soon to join in the shout, "Let him be crucified" (Matt. 27:23).

This shift toward the tragic was already apparent in the prayer the minister prayed following the hymn as we were all settling down in quietness within the sanctuary: "Almighty God, whose most dear Son went not up to joy but first he suffered pain, and entered not into glory before he was crucified: mercifully grant that we, walking in the way of the cross, may find it none other than the way of life and peace; through Jesus Christ our Lord. Amen."[15]

The words "walking in the way of the cross" were ringing in my heart over and over again as I contemplated the spiritual journey of Holy Week, a journey I had begun on Ash Wednesday. I knew that I had come to the most intense part of that pilgrimage—one I could not ignore or take lightly. I realized the events of this week were to order my spiritual experience into a reliving of the spiritual journey experienced by thousands in Jerusalem in the first century. I knew this was not a week for shopping, vacation, parties, or hilarity. I sensed this was the week that above all weeks was to be set aside for the journey into death. I knew the worship of the church would take me by the hand and lead me step-by-step into the experience of death and rebirth, if I would allow it to do so. I resolved then and there to walk in the way of the cross. I purposed to make this the week God intended it to be for me, a week of intense spiritual struggle—and reward!

We stood to read the passion account from Matthew 26:36–27:54. The account had been printed out and each of us had a part: the narrator, Jesus, Pilate, the high priest, Peter, the maid, Judas, Barabbas, and the crowd. All the players were here to reenact the drama. But I was not ready for what was to happen. Only minutes before I was in the crowd at the gate crying and exalting, "Hosanna to the Son of David." But now I was with the same crowd answering Pilate's question, "What shall I do with Jesus who is called the Christ?" by crying, "Let him be crucified" (Matt. 27:22–23). I found myself struggling with those words. I didn't want to say them, but I knew I had to. I knew my sin, even mine, had driven him to the cross. I was a member of both crowds. I had welcomed him into Jerusalem, but like others, I turned on him and drove him to the cross. A hush fell over the entire congregation as we all sensed our own involvement in his death. Together we sank to our knees as we heard the words, "Then he released for them Barabbas, and having scourged Jesus, delivered him to be crucified" (Matt. 27:26).

After a sermon calling us to walk in the way of the cross by making this a special week of spiritual identification with Jesus, the service ended with the Eucharist. Although the music at the Eucharist was sober and oriented around the death of Jesus, there was a glimpse of hope, a light at the end of the tunnel in the words of the eucharistic prayer, "Recalling his death, resurrection and ascension, we offer you these gifts."[16] Again, in the words of the final hymn, I sensed the victory that was to come:

> The royal banners forward go,
> The cross shines forth in mystic glow
> Where he, as man, who gave man breath,
> Now bows beneath the yoke of death.[17]

In the final stanza of that hymn are the reassuring words: "As by the cross thou dost restore." I knew the suffering of Christ was not in vain and that the choice to participate in the suffering of Jesus during this week would lead me to the joy of the resurrection. I also sensed this joy would be more than a mere intellectual idea, that it would be a deep, inner experience in the recesses of my personality. This was the kind of joy that a mere intellectual acquiescence to the resurrection could not create. Only the actual experience of the resurrection through worship, an experience that touched the affective side of my person, could produce that kind of joy.

Monday through Wednesday

Although some churches are open for services on Monday, Tuesday, and Wednesday of Holy Week, most are not. Nevertheless our private devotion during these three days can be ordered by the reading of the lectionary. The Old Testament readings focus on the servant songs of Isaiah and provide us with texts to meditate on the mystery of Christ as the obedient, suffering servant, the servant who gives his life in self-sacrifice yet in the end becomes the victor.

The text for Monday, Isaiah 42:1–7, emphasizes the mission of the servant. He is the one upon whom the Spirit of God rests, and he has come to establish justice. Thus he will open the eyes of the blind and release the prisoners from their dungeons. On Tuesday we are invited to meditate on the commission and call of the Messiah (Isa. 49:1–6). He is the one who will be given as a "light to the nations" so that the salvation of God will reach to the ends of the earth. Then on Wednesday we are brought face-to-face with the passion of our Lord described in great detail in the third reading, Isaiah 50:4–9, "I gave my back to the smiters, and my cheeks to those who pulled out the beard; I hid not my face from shame and spitting" (v. 6).

The Gospel readings prepare us for the betrayal of Jesus and the mounting unbelief of the crowds before his death. On Monday we read of Jesus being anointed by Mary of Bethany and of the scorn heaped on her act of love by Judas, who is called "a thief" (see John 12:1–11). On Tuesday we are asked to meditate on the cause of unbelief (John 12:37–38, 42–50), for the text tells us that even "though he had done so many signs before them, yet they did not believe in him" (v. 37). On Wednesday we are brought closer to the crucifixion as we encounter the disclosure of Judas as the one who will betray Jesus (John 13:21–35). Wednesday is the last full day of Lent. On Thursday at sundown the three great and final days leading to the resurrection will have begun.

Conclusion

We have seen how Lent is the time to die to sin and to the power it holds in our lives. Beginning with Ash Wednesday the call that prevails throughout the Lenten journey is to "create and make in us new and contrite hearts." While it is God who creates that new heart in us through grace, we are called on to receive God's grace in repentance, a turning from our sin, and in faith, a turning toward God. We are assisted in this journey of turning through fasting, prayer, and almsgiving—external disciplines that order and organize the internal experience of our continuing conversion.

The first temptation during Lent will be to break our commitment to walk with God into a new experience of repentance and conversion. Team with another person and enter into an agreement of mutual responsibility and accountability. Keep each other to the agreement made by meeting on a regular basis to review your pilgrimage toward the paschal mystery. I can assure you that if you keep your discipline and enter Holy Week and the Easter mystery with a true spiritual preparation, the power of the resurrection in your own life will exceed your greatest expectations.

Table 6: A Summary of Lenten Spirituality

Theme	Spiritual Emphasis
What is the primary spiritual journey of Lent?	Lent is a time to travel the road with Jesus toward his death.
What is the primary emphasis of Ash Wednesday?	Ash Wednesday begins the journey of Lent. Its theme is repentance and renewal. Ashes are placed on the forehead as a sign of repentance remembering that "from dust you came and to dust you shall return."
What are the Lenten themes for worship and personal spirituality?	The temptation of Christ. Nicodemus' call to abandon pharisaic religion. Say *no* to sin as did the woman of Samaria. Like the man born blind, we can be healed. Prepare for Holy Week.
Why is baptism the metaphor for Lent?	In baptismal spirituality we put off sin and rise to the life of the Spirit. This pattern of spirituality is to live in the death and resurrection of Jesus.
Why does Lent emphasize fasting, prayer, and almsgiving?	Fasting from food is a symbol of the discipline it takes to turn away from sin. Prayer is the act of turning to God in dependence. Almsgiving is the symbol of the virtue we are taking on to replace our sin.
What is a suggested discipline for Lent?	Put off: sloth, faintheartedness, lust of power, and idle talk. Put on: chastity, humility, patience, and love.

A PRAYER FOR LENT

Almighty God, you alone can bring into order the unruly wills and affections of sinners: grant your people grace to love what you have commanded and desire what you promise; that, among the swift and varied changes of the world, our hearts may surely there be fixed where true joys are to be found; through Jesus Christ our Lord, who lives and reigns with you and the Holy Spirit, one God, now and forever. Amen.

From *The Book of Common Prayer*

Questions for Reflection

1. Have you ever practiced a Lenten spirituality? If so, what was your experience? If not, what would you like to gain from a Lenten journey?
2. What is the essence of the Ash Wednesday spiritual experience?
3. How would you apply the Lenten themes to your spiritual journey?
4. Do you live in baptismal spirituality?
5. Have you considered the impact of taking on the disciplines of fasting, prayer, and almsgiving?
6. What do you need to put off? What do you need to put on?

Resources for Lenten Worship and Preaching

Robert Webber, ed., *The Services of the Christian Year*, vol. 5 of *The Complete Library of Christian Worship* (Peabody, MA: Hendrickson, 1994), 225–316.

- Introduction to Lenten worship
- Resources for planning Lenten worship
- The arts in Lenten worship
- Sample services for Lent
- An introduction to Holy Week
- An introduction to Holy Week services
- Worship on Palm/Passion Sunday

THE GREAT TRIDUUM

A Time to Die to Sin

Christ descended into hell to liberate its captives. In one instant he destroyed all record of our ancient debt incurred under the law in order to lead us to heaven where there is no death but only eternal life and righteousness.

Basil of Selencia

A few years ago my parents celebrated their fiftieth wedding anniversary. For all of us in the family, children and grandchildren alike, that event was a gala occasion. There was something very mysterious and powerful about gathering together with these parents who had generated from their loins this fairly large collection of people. For my parents it was a moving memory of an event, now fifty years past, that was made present in that community of people through the songs, the stories, the dramatization, and not least of all the meal that celebrated the event. Somehow that celebration brought all of us to the core event that made the gathering of the Webber offspring possible. It took us back to the point of origin, to the source of it all, so we could memorialize where it all began and recall the meaning of that marriage for all of our lives.

In the Christian year the three great days is that kind of time. It takes the worldwide community of God's offspring back to the originating event and calls on us to enter once again into the meaning of it all. The three great days from Maundy Thursday through the Great Paschal Vigil of Saturday night is the source of our spirituality. Our spiritual journey throughout the year springs from this week, the great paschal mystery of Christ's death and resurrection, and it returns to this week to die with Christ and to be born anew in him.

The season of Lent officially ends on the Thursday evening of Holy Week. Thursday evening begins what the ancient church called the Triduum, or the three great days. These are the days in which we mark the final events of Jesus' life. On Thursday night Jesus instituted the Lord's Supper, washed the feet of his disciples, spoke the new commandment of love, and was arrested. The service that remembers this event is called Maundy (new) Thursday.

Friday is the day on which Christ was crucified. Today his death is remembered with a number of services such as the Seven Last Words and the Veneration of the Cross. On Saturday during the day, the Lord's body rests in repose.

The three great days end with the Great Paschal Vigil, a Saturday night service of fire, Scripture readings, baptism, and the resurrection Eucharist. Lent and the three great days are over. Christ is risen. Alleluia!

While Lent is the journey into the most significant event of human history, the three great days are a life-changing experience of God's saving work in history. For Christians there is no time throughout the entire Christian year that is more crucial than the three great days. These are days to be set aside to enter into a worship that is the source of our entire spirituality, a moment in time that defines all time for Christians, a moment in time that is the very sum and substance of our spirituality for every season, every week, every Sunday, and every moment of every day.

On the Monday after Easter several years ago I stopped by the Wheaton Shoe Shop to have repairs made on a pair of shoes. Knowing that the shoemaker was an ardent Orthodox believer from the old country, I greeted him with "Christ is risen." He turned toward me and lifting a finger heavenward he cried in his deep voice and broken English, "Yes, he is risen every moment of every day!" I sensed that he knew deep in his heart and lived in his life the true meaning of the three great days.

Like the shoemaker, as I have read and meditated on the Triduum texts I have sensed the experience of being drawn into these events themselves. These saving events are not isolated to a time centuries ago in a far-off land and culture. Instead they are evocative events occurring now in my time and place.

The Paschal Triduum (the Three Great Days)

In the ancient church the three days started on Thursday evening and ended with the Great Paschal Vigil of Saturday night. These services are called the Paschal Triduum. These three days are not to be taken lightly or to be frittered away in casual conversation, the search for pleasure, or the pursuit of business. They are the most holy, solemn, and serious days of the entire year. For in these days we experience and encounter our own destiny in the destiny of Christ's ignominious death and burial and in his triumphant resurrection from the dead. If we miss these days we have missed the heart of a full year's spiritual pilgrimage.

Therefore we ought to organize our time and commitments in such a way that absolutely everything during these three days is set aside so we can center entirely and exclusively on our own participation in the death and resurrection of Jesus. Absolutely nothing must be allowed to stand in the way or interfere with the intense spiritual concentration the Triduum demands of us. Of these three great days St. Ambrose, the Bishop of Milan in the fourth century, wrote: "We must observe not only the day of the Passion but the day of the resurrection as well. Thus we will have a day of bitterness and a day of joy; on the one, let us fast, on the other let us seek refreshment . . . during the sacred Triduum . . . [Christ] suffered, rested and rose from the dead. Of that three-day period he himself says: 'Destroy this temple, and in three days I will raise it up.'"[1]

In my own Baptist background there were elements of the seriousness in which these three days were taken. Although the church in which I grew up never had a Maundy Thursday evening service, Good Friday was taken very seriously. There was always a service on Good Friday between noon and three, the hours of our Lord's painful experience on the cross. And Saturday was a very special day spent in preparation for resurrection Sunday. The men of the church always gathered together to build the platform for the sunrise service outside the church, and my mother spent the day preparing for the great feast we always enjoyed with family and friends. These preparations impressed upon me the significance of the three days and left me with an inward sense of their primary importance to my own Christian faith. Even though I wasn't told to feel sober and solemn on Friday and Saturday and full of exuberant joy on Sunday, the three days had a very special feel about them that I can remember to this day. I now know these feelings were evoked by the external preparations we were making for the celebration of those days. I now sense how important external rites are to internal experience.

The early church understood the principle that external rites order internal experience. Consequently the recovery of the early church practices calls us into a deeper and more sensitive relationship to the great paschal mystery. Let me suggest five external practices to help us achieve an inner relationship with these events that give meaning to our spiritual lives. First, be present at all the services of the Great Triduum. Second, observe a total fast after the Maundy Thursday service until after the resurrection service. Third, use this time for quiet meditation and prayer, observing silence as much as possible. Fourth, refrain from shopping, business, and pleasure. Fifth, prepare for the Sunday feast by cleaning house and getting the resurrection feast ready. These external commitments will order the experience of the heart and in a dramatic and real way serve as vehicles for a deep and satisfying experience of the death and resurrection of Jesus, an experience you will recall again and again during the coming year's spiritual journey.

Maundy Thursday

On Maundy Thursday we pass with Jesus into the darkness of his last night, a darkness that will tremble with evil forces—the betrayal, the arrest, the scourging, and his ultimate death on the cross. This is a difficult night, a dark night of the soul in which the determination of Jesus to go to the cross is set in vivid contrast to the powers of evil against which he must struggle. We walk that path with him.

The Agape Meal

In many churches the events of Maundy Thursday begin with the agape feast. For on this night Jesus ate with his disciples, washed their feet, instituted the Last Supper, and was betrayed by Judas. It is a moving experience to begin with the meal, the last meal to be eaten until the Easter meal (when health permits).

The table setting is always austere and the fare is very simple, reminiscent of the foods eaten in the days of Jesus. It consists of freshly baked bread, soup, cheeses, and a variety of nuts and dried fruits with the fruit of the vine to drink. The table prayers are drawn from the ancient Jewish sources that were Christianized in the early centuries of the church. At an appropriate time during the meal the seventeenth chapter of John is read as the people continue to eat in a period of silence. In the quietness of that moment, the prayer Jesus prayed in the Garden of Gethsemane recalls the agony of Jesus as he faced his impending death. As the mood shifts into a more sober realization of our own participation in this event of events, a reader closes the agape meal with a reading from Psalm 69:1–23, which begins, "Save me, O

God! For the waters have come up to my neck." The people then rise and silently move to the sanctuary to continue the pilgrimage into the darkness of a threatening night. With them, I begin to sense in my inner being a centering down of my own soul as it becomes heavy with an identification with Jesus. I move silently with my head lowered to a seat in the sanctuary.

There is no music tonight; the instruments will not sound again until the resurrection service. The quietness of the moment communicates the gravity of the event we have gathered to recall and experience. This is a dark moment in the life of Jesus and in our spirituality, but a most necessary one. The procession is done in silence. The minister turns and solemnly states, "Let us pray. Almighty Father, whose dear Son, on the night before he suffered, instituted the sacrament of His body and blood: mercifully grant that we may receive it thankfully in remembrance of Jesus Christ our Lord, who in these holy mysteries gives us a pledge of eternal life; and who now lives and reigns with you and the Holy Spirit, one God, for ever and ever. Amen."[2]

After the reading of the Scriptures (Exod. 12:1–14; Ps. 78:14–20, 23–25; John 13:1–15; 1 Cor. 11:23–26), the second major act of the evening takes place—the washing of feet.

The Washing of Feet

The practice of foot washing was common in the Eastern world at the time of Christ. Because of the dust in a dry climate and the wearing of sandals, it was natural on entering a home to have your feet washed by one of the servants. The choice Jesus made to wash the feet of his disciples broke the rules of the social order. By assuming the role of the servant, Jesus was already demonstrating the love he would soon express in the humility of the cross—a love and sacrifice that the disciples themselves did not understand. Later Jesus said to them, "A new commandment I give to you, that you love one another; even as I have loved you, that you love one another" (John 13:34).

The term *Maundy* derives its meaning from the Latin *Mandatum Novum*, which means "a new commandment." Thus *Maundy* Thursday is the day Christ instituted the new commandment of love both by word and symbolic action. In the liturgy of the early church the practice of a bishop washing the feet of people over whom he presides is a symbolic action communicating the message that Christianity reverses the social order and calls on all people, especially those who have a higher social position, to see their lives as lives of servanthood. In current worship renewal, this practice is being recovered.

I love to watch this ancient custom reenacted. Several members of the congregation, representing different age levels, may walk forward and sit in a place where they can be seen. The minister, picking up a bowl of water and placing a freshly laundered towel over his or her shoulder, bends to wash the feet of each of the persons one by one, lifting each foot and kissing it as was done in the ancient church. During this action portions of John 13:1–5 are read with the choir responding: "Peace is my last gift to you, my own peace I now leave with you; peace which the world cannot give, I give to you." As the feet of the last person are washed the reader ends with the words, "By this shall the world know that you are my disciples: that you have love for one another."[3]

Silence is kept for a minute or more as the meaning of both words and the symbolic action are allowed to sink more deeply into one's consciousness. As I meditate on the meaning of Jesus washing the feet of his disciples, I am reminded once again that my calling in life is to be a servant, a person who like Jesus is willing to give my life in self-sacrificing love to the service of others. My own spirituality is to be ordered by Jesus' example. I am to serve my wife and children, my students, and my colleagues. My calling is not "What can you do for me?" but "What can I do for you?" This attitude reflects the Spirit of Christ, the same Spirit who is to be in us in all our relationships. Maundy Thursday is a good time to review this calling to live by self-sacrificing love and to examine our own lives in relationship to the message of self-giving love, a message that is to order our spirituality through the year.

The Institution of the Lord's Supper

On the night before our Lord was betrayed by Judas he instituted the Lord's Supper, an act that comes after the foot washing in the service of Maundy Thursday. The setting for the supper is the Passover feast of the Jews that Jesus was celebrating with his disciples (Matt. 26:17–29). In that context he took the bread, blessed it, broke it, and gave it to his disciples saying, "Take, eat; this is my body" (v. 26). Then taking the cup he gave thanks again and said, "Drink of it, all of you; for this is my blood of the covenant, which is poured out for many for the forgiveness of sins" (vv. 27–28). In this simple action he took the central Jewish festival that marked Jewish spirituality and transformed it into a major source of Christian spirituality. In that action the bread and wine became the Christian Passover, the sign of the new covenant of salvation established through the death and resurrection of Jesus.

In the Maundy Thursday celebration we recall the *institution* of the Lord's Supper. It is a sober reminder of the connection made between bread, wine, and death. We are reminded that the death of Jesus is no mere human tragedy but a voluntary suffering by Jesus to be a sacrifice for us. He died to take away the condemnation against us for our sin.

It is common in the ancient church to celebrate not only the death but also the resurrection in our table worship. On this night our spirituality is ordered into a deep, intense, and sustained emphasis on the death of Christ. The service asks us to recall that this is the "night when he was betrayed" (1 Cor. 11:23).

Because worship is not simply a record of the past but a means through which the past is made present, we are truly there. In the quietness of this moment, the liturgy asks us to see our own sin as we have betrayed Christ. We may say that we love him and we may attend the liturgy regularly and participate in the life of the church, yet does not our indifference to Christ's claim over our lives and our failure to truly live by Christian values speak of our betrayal? The Great Triduum calls us to an *identification* with Christ and his suffering. Whatever else can be said about Judas, I sense the burden of betrayal he felt, a burden that led him to such anguish and remorse that he killed himself. But Jesus died to pay the penalty for the sin of Judas, to release Judas from condemnation and restore him to a relationship with Christ.

We are to bring our own Judas to the table of the Lord. The cup that we drink is the cup of Jesus' blood poured out for the forgiveness of our sins. It is a covenant drink and food. We have offended our holy God by our sins, and his wrath demands a punishment for that offense. But Jesus, by his voluntary death, offers to take upon himself our sins so that God will forgive us. When we eat the bread and drink the wine we say, "Jesus' death was for *me*, I accept the fact that I am now reconciled to God through the sacrifice of Jesus." On this night we come face-to-face in a fresh way with the message that we cannot find peace with God through our own works or moral goodness. We can only trust in Jesus who died for us to set us free.

On this night as we stand to walk forward, as we stretch forth our hands to receive the symbol of his broken body, and as we lift our lips to receive the sign of his blood shed for us, we ought to ask God to order our spiritual pilgrimage now and for the next several days into a deep centering on his death. For until Easter when we celebrate the resurrection, the focus of our spiritual journey is into the very heart of God's own suffering, which Jesus endured for our sake.

The Solemn Stripping of the Table

The final act of the Maundy Thursday service is the solemn stripping of the communion table, which symbolizes stripping Jesus of his garments in preparation for the crucifixion (Matt. 27:31). This sign brings us into a deeper encounter with the suffering and ignominy that Jesus embraced for us.

The service of the Eucharist is now over; the ministers along with other members of the community silently and soberly wash the communion table with water. At the same time others strip the table and other parts of the space of all signs of life and color. Flowers, lamps, candles, cushions, tablecloths, and all forms of beauty are carried out of the church and put into a closet until the day of the resurrection. As these actions are taking place the congregation says or sings Psalm 22, which concludes with the antiphon, "They divide my garments among them and cast lots for my clothing" (v. 18 NIV).

In many churches the sanctuary remains open all night for people to come and pray. There may be a sign-up sheet for people to pray for a half hour or full hour between the closing of Maundy Thursday and sunrise. This symbolizes the disciples who stayed with Jesus in the Garden of Gethsemane until the betrayal by Judas took place and Jesus was apprehended by his accusers.

Because our spirituality is ordered by the events of Maundy Thursday, it is of great spiritual value to voluntarily experience this time of prayer and meditation. While many persons cannot and should not stay up all night, choosing to disturb the pattern of sleep to pray with Jesus is a powerful way to feel and experience the suffering of Jesus in our own bodies and spirit. It is important that we avoid a mere intellectual recalling of Jesus' pain. Unless we actually subject our bodies and stomach to a meaningful discipline, the actual sense of experiencing Christ's suffering will elude us. As our bodies become tired and our muscles begin to ache, our eyes to burn, our stomachs to hunger, and our spirits to grow dim, we begin to experience in a physical and psychological way a touch of our Lord's pain. This physical and spiritual sadness is a way of actually entering into Christ's death in an empathetic way creating a sense of our spiritual oneness with him.[4]

Good Friday

It is a matter of interest that the day of the Lord's death is called *Good* Friday. In terms of Jesus' own pain and suffering, it was not a good day. But in view of the death of Jesus as a day when the powers of evil were put to flight and dethroned, it was indeed a *good* day. Our celebration of that day in worship captures the tension of both the sorrow we bring to the day through our identification with Jesus and the joy we experience knowing that his death was the death of death, the ruination of the powers of evil.

In the early church the worship of Good Friday was always seen as a continuation of the worship begun the evening before and continued through the night. In fourth-century Jerusalem the Christians who had been worshiping all night processed from the Garden of Gethsemane and arrived in Jerusalem as the sun was rising. Here the trial before Pilate was read and prayers were said at the place where it was believed Jesus was scourged. After the prayers people went home for a brief rest, returning again in the late morning for a service venerating the wood of the cross. A piece of wood, believed by some to be a relic from the cross, was placed on a white linen before the bishop. As the people filed by they touched or kissed the wood of the cross as a way of expressing their devotion to Christ, who was slain on the cross.

Then between noon and three they gathered again to hear lessons about Jesus' death through a variety of Scripture readings. At three they ended the service with a reading of the death of Jesus from one of the Gospels. Again in the evening they gathered to hear the reading of the burial, many of them staying on through the night to pray and meditate on the meaning of his death. For them the recalling of the events of Jesus' life on that day ordered their spiritual pilgrimage into an identification with him in the hour of his death.

Today there are at least three different services on Good Friday that recreate these events. While no church will do all of these services each year, many churches will conduct one or more of these services on a Good Friday, allowing the worshiper over several years to order his or her spirituality by each service. These services include the Way of the Cross, the Three Hours Devotion, and the Veneration of the Cross.

The Way of the Cross

This service, sometimes called the Stations of the Cross, probably arose in Jerusalem where Christians marked out the last journey of Jesus from Pilate's house to Calvary. Their purpose was to identify with Jesus by participating spiritually in the final events of his life. Throughout the centuries the Stations of the Cross went through a number of changes until it was standardized in the seventeenth century into fourteen stations. Nine of these scenes are drawn from the actual Gospel accounts and five from popular tradition. Because it ends with Christ in the tomb, some churches are adding a resurrection scene. When the devotion is used on Good Friday or anytime during Lent or Holy Week, it is preferable not to add a resurrection station, leaving the resurrection proclamation for the service on Easter Sunday.

The Way of the Cross is a moving service that is best used on the morning of Good Friday. The service is especially stirring if you have been following Jesus through the night and now continue to follow him in the final events of his life. You can do the service privately by prayerfully meditating slowly on each of the stations, or you can usually find a church nearby that conducts a public celebration of the service. (Catholic and Episcopal churches are especially likely to have such services.)

I have celebrated this service many times, but each time it brings me into a fresh encounter with the journey of Jesus into death. In every step of that journey I carry with me my Lenten experience and my commitment to change from a servanthood to the evil one into living in the likeness of Christ. When Jesus is condemned to death, then nailed to the cross, and finally placed in the grave, I experience my sins being placed upon him, nailed to the cross with him, and finally buried with him in the grave. In this way the Stations of the Cross service readies me more intensely for an internal experience of the resurrection soon to come.[5]

The Three Hours Devotion

Like the Way of the Cross service, the Three Hours Devotion is designed to help the worshiper identify with Jesus. Here the devotion becomes more intense because it presents the last words of Jesus as a way of ordering spirituality into the suffering Jesus endured on the cross. The origin of this service goes all the way back to fourth-century Jerusalem, as do most devotions surrounding the three great days. The time between noon and three in the afternoon when Jesus hung on the cross was set aside for various Scripture readings related to the passion, interspersed with prayers and ending with the reading of the passion story from John's Gospel.

The particular shape of today's Three Hours Devotion originated in Peru in the latter part of the seventeenth century and concentrated on the seven last words of Christ. It spread first among Catholic churches, then to the Anglican church, and through the Anglicans to various Protestant churches.

I recommend you attend this service in silence and allow these final words to sink deep into your consciousness by centering on their meaning. Identify with Jesus on this day and go the whole journey with him to the cross, and hang as it were with him, entering into his pain and suffering. Allow this experience to shape your devotion and create within you the pattern of dying with Christ through a physical identification with him. By fasting from food, pleasure, and business as usual, you will be able to feel Christ's death in your muscles, in your stomach, in the weariness of your body, and in your silence.

The Veneration of the Cross

Like the Way of the Cross and the Three Hours Devotion, the Veneration of the Cross also originated in Jerusalem in the fourth century. It was popularized in Jerusalem in the seventeenth century and handed down through Catholic and Anglican piety. This service, which is usually done on Friday night, consists of three parts: the service of the Word with the intercessions, the veneration of the cross, and holy communion.

The service begins in absolute silence as the people quietly take their seats and bow or kneel in preparation. The ministers, robed in black, silently process to the table and either stand quietly with heads bowed or kneel or prostrate themselves on the floor for a brief period of time. After a prayer the readings from Scripture commence. First Isaiah 52:13–53:12 is read followed by a responsive reading of Psalm 22:1–22; then Hebrews 4:14–16; 5:7–9 is read. Finally the passion according to John 18:1–19:42 is read or sung. A brief period of silence is kept between each reading as the faithful meditate on the readings. Sometimes a brief sermon is preached.

Now comes the intercession. On this occasion the prayers of intercession are longer than usual and cover the whole range of intercessory prayer. Prayers are lifted up for the entire church, for all nations and peoples of the earth, for peace, for those who suffer, and for those who have not received the gospel. What better time than at the hour of his death for us to acknowledge Christ as the one who hears our prayers, for his death is surely a response to the cry of affliction we feel on account of sin. Surely he who went to the cross to bear our sins will hear us when we pray. These prayers of intercession at the foot of the cross make me sense the extent of Christ's victory over death. He who died to conquer death lives to overcome the power of evil in all people and everywhere in his world. The prayers of intercession touch me with a powerful sense of the resurrection that is to come and give me hope in the midst of the great day of sorrow.

Next comes the veneration of the cross. This may be a difficult part of the service for many Protestants if they misunderstand veneration. Several years ago I was asked to conduct the Good Friday service sponsored by the ministerial association of Wheaton. I chose to do the Veneration of the Cross service. After the intercessions I gave a brief sermon on the meaning of veneration. "In a few minutes," I said, "a veiled cross will be carried up the aisle and unveiled in three steps. The person carrying the cross will walk one third of the way into the sanctuary carrying the cross. He will stop, unveil the left side of the cross, lift the cross high, and sing, 'This is the wood of the cross on which hung the Savior of the world,' to which you will sing, 'Thanks be to God.' The third time this is done the cross will be in the front of the church near the table of the Lord. You will be invited one by one to leave your seat, come stand before the cross for a moment, touch it if you wish or even kneel and kiss it. You are not venerating a piece of wood. You are honoring Christ who hung on the cross, the instrument of our salvation."

In that service containing Protestants of every denomination more than two thirds of the people there, people who had never before venerated the cross, came down to touch or kiss the wood of the cross as the choir sang the three prescribed anthems and Scriptures were read. As I touched the wood of the cross I felt as though I was coming into contact with the hard fact of death. What Jesus did for me was made real. He died on the hard wood of the cross, nailed to that cross in pain and agony. I felt as though I was in touch with the hard, brutal, historical fact of a crucified Jesus, and I lifted my heart in grateful thanks to the one who died for me, to set me free from the power of sin in my own life.

Finally the Eucharist, taken on this day from the bread consecrated on Thursday night and received in quietness without the normal prayers of thanksgiving, ends the service. In quietness we leave, for Jesus has been placed in the tomb.[6]

Holy Saturday

In most churches there is no Holy Saturday service. When there is, it is generally in the morning and consists of Scripture readings and prayers. However, the Great Paschal Vigil service, to which I will turn shortly, may start late on Saturday night (10 PM) or early on Sunday morning (5 AM).

Saturday is a day of rest and preparation for the great service of resurrection. It is a day to keep silence, to fast, to pray, to identify with Jesus in the tomb, and to prepare for the great resurrection feast.

The Easter Vigil

In my evangelical background Christmas was the primary Christian event, not Easter. However, in the ancient church the opposite was true. The celebration of the three great days of death and resurrection culminated in an all-night Easter service known as the Great Paschal Vigil.

Of course we need both Christmas and Easter. There is no death and resurrection without the incarnation. Nevertheless the very center of our faith is found in the events of the three great days, and the greatest of these days is the glorious and wondrous day of the resurrection. For on this day the new day of the re-creation of the world has begun.

This theme of "re-creation," of the "beginning again," of the "new day" runs through the entire Easter vigil and throughout the entire seven weeks of the Easter season. The vigil itself is made up of four services: First, there is the service of light proclaiming the new beginning. Second, in a service of readings the entire history of salvation is proclaimed. Third, in the service of baptism the new beginning is expressed in the sign of our identity with Jesus. Finally, the celebration of the Easter Eucharist is an experience of the new life in Christ.

The Service of Light

My first experience of the Easter vigil service occurred in the early seventies. Easter in the previous year had been a huge disappointment. I had attended an early sunrise service that was very ordinary. The only visual symbol was a large cross, which I very much appreciated. But the service itself was a typical Sunday service with "Up from the Grave He Arose," an exuberant choir rendition of several resurrection songs, and a long, tedious sermon on the evidences for the resurrection. I vowed then and there that Easter would be different for me the next year.

I had heard about the Saturday Great Paschal Vigil service from an acquaintance, so I made my way to a church that celebrated this service. I pushed open the front door of the church and found myself in a large, dark vestibule full of people. It was a very dark space, so I huddled near the door where I had entered knowing I was surrounded by people and fearing to move lest I bump into someone. I simply stood there in the dark and waited.

I didn't know it at the time, but being in the dark was laden with significance. In the ancient world where there was no electricity the day and the night were regulated by the setting and rising of the sun. The use of light to dispel darkness in both the Jewish and Christian traditions was filled with meaning. In this case the service of the Great Paschal Vigil began in the dark because the light of Christ had been extinguished by his death.

After what seemed like a very long time, the darkness was dramatically broken as a match was lit and thrown into a Weber kettle full of kindling wood. Immediately the whole narthex was lit, and I could see the faces of the people. Instantly the worship leader sang out, "The Light of Christ," to which the people responded, "Thanks be to God."

A new, large candle known as the paschal candle was lit. (This candle will be used throughout the year to represent the resurrected Christ in the midst of his people. It will be extinguished on Good Friday of the next year when the world dwells in darkness again.) The service then continued as the entire congregation processed into the dark sanctuary, which gradually reflected the light of all the candles as they flickered in the sanctuary and cast their new light on the walls of the church. During the procession the cantor sang the "Exalted," a historic song I had never heard before. This great hymn of the church begins, "Rejoice, now, all heavenly choirs of angels." It then continues to express the deep theological meaning of this very special night. This is the night of the new Passover, the night when darkness becomes light, sadness becomes joy, despair becomes hope, death becomes life. The content of this great proclamation and the symbolic context of darkness turning into light impressed upon me how truly life-changing the resurrection is. I was also reminded how important it is for us to find a way in the symbolic world in which we live to express this great truth in a new and unforgettable way.

The Service of the Readings

The service now transitioned to a number of readings from Scripture. Between the readings we sang hymns, songs, antiphons, and the like. Since I knew nothing about this service, I was unaware that in the ancient church Scriptures were read throughout the night and ended at dawn with the service of baptism. Today the ancient length of the service generally is not followed. The Scripture readings will vary from church to church and will take anywhere from thirty minutes to an hour. The purpose of these readings is to recount the history of God's salvation throughout the Old Testament and to focus on Jesus as the fulfillment of all these passages and prophecies.

The readings speak of God's creation, of the fall, and of how God became involved in history to save creatures and creation. The readings end with the accounts of the death and resurrection of Jesus. I remember, as an evangelical, thinking of how special this was on this primal night of faith to recount the whole story of the gospel. Years later a woman who was involved in a church that celebrated the Great Paschal Vigil told me her nine-year-old daughter turned to her during the readings and whispered, "Mommy, don't you just love these stories?" She was shocked that a nine-year-old knew what was going on! In our postmodern world it is imperative that we recover the story of faith. Here is a service that will lodge that story in our memory. Done in the context of a dimly lit church, spoken in reverence and responded to in joy, this is a service that cannot be forgotten. It has a way of recounting truth so that it takes up residence within and shapes us into the continuation of the story.

The Service of Baptism

The third part of the Great Paschal Vigil is the service of baptism. I knew nothing about the ancient baptismal practices at the time, but I have since studied the practice of baptism in the early church and its translation into the contemporary world. Those who are to be baptized have gone through a long process in preparation for their baptism on the day of the resurrection. The length of preparation in the early church was generally two or three years. In today's world the time of preparation is most often a year or less. No matter how long it takes, this is a very special night.

Those to be baptized have taken a spiritual journey into faith, followed by a long period of discipleship and spiritual formation. During the time of preparation, these soon-to-be-baptized persons have been dismissed after the sermon to go with an instructor to reflect on the teaching of the faith as the rest of the community prays together, passes the peace, and receives the Eucharist. They have learned the disciplines of the faith—how to pray, read Scripture, discern spiritual warfare, and care for the needs of the poor, the weak, and the homeless. They have also been integrated into the life of the church, and tonight, after their baptism, they will be received into the full life of the church.

As their names are called, those to be baptized come up front with their mentors. They are asked again, "Do you reject Satan and all that is sin and death?" Then comes the question of faith once again, "Do you turn to Jesus Christ as your Lord and Savior?" After answering these questions in the affirmative, they are invited to "enter the tomb" of Christ to receive the water of baptism. Kneeling in the waters, the converting persons are baptized into the name of the Father, the Son, and the Holy Spirit as the Apostles' Creed is proclaimed to express their faith in the Triune God.

As they come out of the water the newly baptized kneel again for another rite. This time oil is poured over their heads. It streams down their face into their eyes and mouth. The minister spreads the oil gently and lovingly over the entire face and head of the newly baptized as they smell the fragrance of the oil that represents the sweet presence of the Holy Spirit given to form their lives into a continuing relationship with Jesus Christ. Now a candle is lit from the Christ candle and given to them to remind them that they bear the light of Christ and are to be witnesses to him in all of their lives. They are then given a white gown and told to go change into this Easter dress of white raiment and return after changing to join with the whole church to receive the Easter Eucharist to celebrate the resurrection and their new life in Christ.[7]

My baptism at age twelve was a very special event in my own life. My father, the pastor, asked, "Do you reject the devil and all his works?" "Do you turn to Jesus as your Lord and Savior?" Those words of *metanoia* still ring in my ears and heart. Whenever anyone asks me to give a testimony of faith, I always go back to this baptismal rite. I see it not only as my conversion rite but the event that calls me into a continual repentance of faith, a rite for every moment of every day.

Recent studies in life-changing rites show that they are made up of three elements: (1) a renunciation of a former way of life, (2) a transition, and (3) a transformation of life. My own baptism was a turning point but done without a great deal of ceremony. It makes me realize that a powerful baptism done on resurrection Sunday may become a life-transforming event and a lifelong spiritual memory.

I don't remember all the details of that first vigil I attended, but I do remember the spiritual fuss made over the newly baptized in the eucharistic service that followed the baptism. They were introduced to the congregation as they stood before them in their new, white robes; they carried the bread and wine in a procession to the table; they were served bread and wine first and then served the bread and wine to others. After the service they were honored again at the resurrection banquet held in the fellowship hall of the church. When a person has been truly born of the Spirit and goes through these rites in a meaningful manner, they remain in his or her conscious memory as the turning point of life.

In today's world where the longing for rites and symbols as markers of life transitions are sought out, I can think of no sign of the new birth that compares with the biblical sign of baptism. Baptism is the image of the transition to a full, conscious, and active life in the community of Christ's body on earth.

The Service of Eucharist

The Great Paschal Vigil ends with a eucharistic celebration that will not soon be forgotten. It is just the opposite of what I experienced in that early morning sunrise service that compelled me to find something different. Instead of presenting the evidences for the resurrection, the Holy Spirit speaks to the heart and the senses and confirms truth. The most memorable sermon I have heard in the Easter celebration consisted of seven words. The minister cried, "He is risen," and the people responded in a shout, "He is risen indeed." At that moment the organist burst forth with the sounds of "Alleluia!" and all the people sang "Alleluia!" in response. The bells of the church began to ring loudly, and from everywhere people came with potted lilies so that in one single moment the sanctuary was filled with the flowers of new life. Through sound and sight the church had passed from the stillness of death to the reverberations of life that filled the sanctuary with praise. Then the whole community proceeded to sing the "Gloria in Excelsis Deo." The Eucharist proceeded as a usual Sunday Eucharist (every Sunday is a little Easter), but it was very special because it was the day of the resurrection.

Conclusion

In this chapter I have presented the three great days of salvation—Maundy Thursday, Good Friday, and the Saturday night Great Paschal Vigil. Christian spirituality is ultimately based on these events because they commemorate real events of God happening in space and time in which Jesus Christ was crucified for our sins and was resurrected for our new life. They are the events that establish our spirituality. Also, because our spirituality is *in* Jesus Christ, we are to live in these events through our continual dying to sin and our ever rising to the life of the Spirit. Therefore it is imperative for the church to go beyond its present practice to recover the fullness of the three great days and to impress upon us all how important these days are, not only as historical events to be remembered but as events to be lived in our own dying to sin and rising to the life of the Spirit. For herein lies the source and energy of our spiritual lives.

Table 7: A Summary of the Three Great Days Spirituality

Theme	Spiritual Emphasis
What are the three great days of history?	Maundy Thursday Good Friday Holy Saturday (ending in the resurrection)
Why are these three days so crucial to spirituality?	The death and resurrection of Jesus is the **source** of our spirituality. These days constitute the pattern of our living-dying to sin, rising to the life of the Spirit.
What does Maundy Thursday recall?	The Last Supper The washing of the feet The arrest of Jesus
What services recall the death of Christ on Good Friday?	The Way of the Cross The Three Hours Devotion The Veneration of the Cross

Continued

What are the four services of the Easter vigil?	The service of light
	The service of readings
	Baptism
	Resurrection Eucharist

A PRAYER FOR TRIDUUM

O God, who for our redemption didst give thine only-begotten Son to the death of the cross, and by his glorious resurrection hast delivered us from the power of our enemy: grant us to die daily to sin, that we may evermore live with him in the joy of his resurrection; through the same thy Son Christ our Lord, who liveth and reigneth with thee and the Holy Spirit, one God, now and forever, Amen.

From *The Book of Common Prayer*

Questions for Reflection

1. Take time to contemplate on God's mighty acts of salvation as the source of your spirituality.
2. How have you entered into his death this past year? What sins in your life need to be brought to death?
3. How have you been raised to new life in his resurrection this past year? In what ways do you wish to be brought into renewal this next year?

Resources for Triduum Worship and Preaching

See Robert Webber, ed., *The Services of the Christian Year*, vol. 5 of *The Complete Library of Christian Worship* (Peabody, MA: Hendrickson, 1994), 381–96.

- Resources for worship on Maundy Thursday
- Resources for worship on Good Friday
- Resources for worship of other services of Holy Week
- Resources for the Great Paschal Vigil

7

EASTER

A Time to Be Resurrected

The festival we celebrate today is one of victory—the victory of the Son of God, King of the whole universe. On this day the devil is defeated by the crucified one; our race is filled with joy by the risen one.

Hesychius of Jerusalem

Before I learned about the Christian year, Easter was a one-day event, not a seven-week season. Of course this one-day event was very special. I remember as a child the preparation made in our home for Easter. In those days, sixty years ago, the emphasis was on a *new day,* and one of the primary ways to celebrate this new day was with new clothing. The purchase of new clothing to be worn on Easter Sunday morning may seem very strange in today's culture where "dressing up for God" has been replaced with a "come as you are" dress code.

I don't know that I even thought about the meaning of wearing something new for Easter, nor do I know where the tradition came from. Perhaps it is related to the book of Revelation in which St. John refers to those "who have not soiled their clothes. They will walk with me, dressed in white, for they are worthy. He who overcomes will, like them, be dressed in white" (Rev. 3:4–5 NIV). My new clothing always included something white—a new white shirt, white trousers, or both. This was true of almost all the people in Montgomery Baptist Church.

141

On the Sunday of Easter nearly everyone wore something white—a white dress, white suit, white hat, white shirt, white trousers, white shoes.

White is a powerful symbol of something special! Children wear beautiful white garments for their moment of dedication or baptism; gorgeous white gowns are worn to celebrate a marriage; white clothes are worn in the spring to proclaim that winter is over, the sun is out, the earth is being warmed, the flowers are blooming, the trees are budding, the bushes are green, and the grass is growing. White is the color of Easter and of the resurrection, for it is the color of new, clean, and set apart. In the early church, perhaps influenced by the writing of Revelation, those who were baptized at the Great Paschal Vigil wore a white robe on Easter Sunday and on all the Sundays of Easter.

In the Christian year, Easter is indeed an event—the event of the glorious resurrection of Jesus from the dead. But as I mentioned at the beginning of this chapter, Easter is not a single day; it is a season that lasts until Pentecost.

There is biblical precedent for Easter as a season. After the resurrection Jesus appeared to his disciples over a period of forty days, teaching them the truths of the kingdom (Acts 1:3). On the fortieth day he ascended into heaven. Ten days later the Holy Spirit descended upon them (Acts 2:1–47). Following the history of the postresurrection period, Easter developed into a seven-week celebration that included the ascension and ended with the coming of the Spirit on the day of Pentecost. We turn now to look at Easter as the season of white and the season to celebrate the resurrection, the ascension, and the coming of the Holy Spirit on the day of Pentecost. This is a great season for the spiritual formation of every Christian.

Easter Day

I have always been trained to think of the resurrection as a historic fact, and indeed, it is. Paul clearly states the factual reality to the Corinthian church. It appears that some Corinthian Christians denied the Easter fact but affirmed the Easter faith. To them Paul wrote, "But if it is preached that Christ has been raised from the dead, how can some of you say that there is no resurrection of the dead? If there is no resurrection of the dead, then not even Christ has been raised. And if Christ has not been raised, our preaching is useless and so is your faith" (1 Cor. 15:12–14 NIV).

Some theologians at the turn of the century (and some today) deny the Easter fact but affirm the Easter faith. *What Is Christianity?* by Adolf Harnack was published at the turn into the twentieth century. In his book Harnack proclaimed that we must hold the Easter faith even in the absence of the Easter fact.[1]

My background—my upbringing, my education, and the evangelical circles in which I have lived my life—is very strong on the Easter fact. We are offended by all who reject it. Consequently, we have garnered all the evidences for the resurrection as fact to win over those who deny the resurrection or find it a stumbling block to faith. But in our earnestness to defend the Easter fact, I wonder if we have so intellectualized the resurrection that it has become fact and not faith—or at least a weakened and misunderstood faith.

I remember an Easter sermon given more than thirty years ago by my Wheaton College colleague Morris Inch. He raised the questions: Have we evangelicals so thoroughly defended the Easter fact that we have lost the power and significance of the Easter faith? Are we missing the meaning of the resurrection in our own lives? Are we no longer conscious of the pattern of death and resurrection in our own lives? Do we no longer expect resurrections to occur in our own lives?

I was stunned. He was speaking to me. I was so focused on defending the fact that Jesus had truly and historically risen from the dead that I never consciously thought about my own need to follow the pattern of Jesus, to die to sin in him and to be raised in him to the resurrected life of the Spirit. This was a sermon that set in motion a kind of thinking that did not lessen my embrace of the resurrection as a fact, but it certainly intensified my concern not only that the resurrection of Jesus happened in a particular place and time in history but also that the resurrection must happen *in me*.

You Have Been Raised with Christ

The notion that Christ must be resurrected in us is a primary theme for Easter Sunday. Indeed the personal dimension of the entire Christian year flows from this subjective experience of the Easter event. If Christ has truly been raised in us, then we can experience the waiting of Advent and the joy of Christmas. We can become an epiphany. We can truly walk the Lenten road and the three great days as an experience of a truly spiritual journey of transformation. We can become an Easter person and a Pentecost presence.

Easter is the source event of all the events of the Christian year. It is like the neck of the hourglass. Every event of the Christian year flows into Easter, even as all the events of the Christian year flow from Easter.

Evangelicals affirm that Easter day, like all the other saving events of the Christian year, is a factual and historical day. On Easter Sunday the two sides of the Easter event are to be affirmed. When Easter day is reduced only to a fact day, we intellectualize the event. If I focus only on the evidence of the resurrection fact, the reality of the resurrection in me is removed and the meaning of the resurrection spirituality becomes lost.

There is also a danger, however, in overinterpreting the resurrection event in me. We live in a highly self-focused world in which everything is interpreted in terms of what it can do for me. Greg Wilde, a friend of mine and a teacher at the Institute for Worship Studies, captured the concentration on self that has become a real problem for the church and its emphasis on true spirituality in the following way:

> In all past paradigms the self has been subordinated to systems—moral systems, social systems, political systems, even physical systems, like gravity and environmental conditions. In the last 30 years, however, or perhaps gradually since the second World War, for the first time the self has been cut loose to become supreme, sovereign, all-important, a system unto itself, no longer subordinate to any moral code but its own, no longer needing anybody outside the self, no longer needing to agree with anybody to receive validation, and even technology has advanced to the point where we no longer have to obey gravity, or stay above water or even stay on the planet! We can do anything and it has killed us.[2]

While the resurrection is for me, it is not a *self-focused* event as in advertising that states, "It is all about me, you know!" Maintaining the paradox of both the Easter fact and faith is the key to Easter spirituality. Paul clearly provides the subjective guideline: "You have been raised with Christ. . . . Your life is now hidden with Christ in God" (Col. 3:1, 3 NIV). So what does it mean to say that Christ has been factually risen from the dead and this same Christ is to be risen in me? What is the Easter message? The answer to this question must focus first on the Easter fact and then, and only then, on Easter spirituality.

The Easter Fact

Before it is possible to clearly state how we participate in the resurrection, the meaning of the resurrection must be made clear. The Easter message, according to the ancient church fathers' interpretation of Scripture, is that the entire creation has been renewed. The fact of the resurrection is that God won a victory over the powers of evil—those powers that seek to destroy God's creation. The story of the victory of Christ over evil goes all the way back to the fall and the prediction made in Genesis 3:15, "I will put enmity between you and the woman, and between your offspring and hers; *he will crush your head, and you will strike his heel*" (NIV, italics added).

For the early church fathers, Easter day is the day of *Christus Victor*. Melito of Sardis (AD 195) preached this theme in his great Easter sermon:

> But he rose from the dead and mounted up to the heights of heaven. When the Lord had clothed himself with humanity and had suffered for the sake of the sufferer, and had been bound for the sake of the imprisoned, and had been judged for the sake of the condemned, and buried for the sake of the one who was buried, he rose from the dead, and cried with a loud voice: Who is he that contends with me? Let him stand in opposition to me. I set the condemned man free; I gave the dead man life; I raised up one who had been entombed. Who is my opponent? I, he says, am the Christ. *I am the one who destroys death and triumphed over the enemy and trampled Hades underfoot and bound the strong one*, and carried off man to the heights of heaven. I, he says, am the Christ.[3]

Easter day is the day that confirms the mission of God accomplished. God has reclaimed creation. He is Lord over the powers that rage against him and seek to destroy his created order.

The Bible tells us the story of the world. The story is that God's good creation has been corrupted by the fall. Creatures are so deeply wounded and turned in on themselves that they are unable to repair the damage made by Adam and inherited by the whole human race. The impact of this disastrous human condition is so thoroughly expressed within creation that "the whole creation has been groaning" (Rom. 8:22 NIV) because of its "subjection to frustration" (Rom. 8:20 NIV). The most dramatic element of this story is that God became incarnate in Jesus in order to reverse the human situation. Paul captures this great cosmic reversal in Romans 5:18: "Consequently, just as the result of one trespass was condemnation for all men, so also the result of one act of righteousness was justification that brings life for all men" (NIV). The work of Christ in overcoming evil extends beyond creatures to all creation. For "the creation itself will be liberated from its bondage to decay and brought into the glorious freedom of the children of God" (Rom. 8:21 NIV). Melito shows how the day of Easter brings together creation, fall, incarnation, death and suffering, resurrection victory, and the eschatological hope of humanity in the re-creation of all things. In a few striking sentences he tells this sweeping story and captures the message of the Easter fact. The fact is that God has reversed the fallen human situation.

In the incarnation God became the second Adam. The first Adam brought sin into the world, but the second Adam brought righteousness; the first Adam brought death into the world, but the second Adam brought life; the first Adam brought condemnation, but the second Adam brought justification. Therefore, Jesus Christ, the new man, completely renewed the face of the earth. Through his life he sanctified life; in his death he paid the penalty of sin and made man right with God; in his resurrection he broke the power of death and opened the way to heaven and to a new life for the whole world. The church is now called to be a witness to the new beginning brought to the world through Jesus Christ. The church is called to embody this Easter fact by being the new creation and calling people into its new life as it awaits the second coming of Jesus to destroy all the powers and reign as Lord over all creation. This is the Easter fact, and our hope for the new creation is grounded in Easter Sunday. Herein lies the source and meaning of our Easter spirituality.

Easter Spirituality

Christ is the one in whom life and the new creation, the beginning again of our lives and all of creation, is assured. Our Easter calling is to let him live in us, to embrace by faith his new life, to let it take hold of us, to participate in him and his resurrection for the life of the whole world. In this way we are born again (John 3:3); we are made a new creation (2 Cor. 5:17).

The biblical metaphor for Easter spirituality is found in baptism. The baptized life is a life that is lived in the *pattern of death and resurrection*. The burden of Paul is to show that baptism pictures the two sides of our spiritual lives—death to evil and resurrection to the life of the Spirit. Paul's signature passage on Easter spirituality is found in Romans 6: "We were therefore buried with him through baptism [Lent is the road that leads to the baptismal burial] into death in order that, just as Christ was raised from the dead [Easter is the event of our baptismal resurrection] through the glory of the Father, we too may live a new life" (v. 4 NIV). Now Paul reaches his punch line: "If we have been united with him like this in his death, we will certainly also be united with him in his resurrection" (v. 5 NIV). The concept of *union* is clearly the subjective element of Christ *in me*. The idea here is very concrete; there is no missing the point. In union with his death we are to die to sin. In union with his resurrection, we are to live a new life. "For we know that our old self was crucified with him so that the body of sin might be done away with, that we should no longer be slaves to sin—because anyone who has died has been freed from sin" (vv. 6–7 NIV). The victory of Christ breaks the powers of evil that lead us to sin. We no longer need to yield to the temptations and attractions of the powers of evil. "Now if we died with Christ, we believe that we will also live with him. For we know that since Christ was raised from the dead, he cannot die again;

death no longer has mastery over him. . . . Count yourselves dead to sin but alive to God in Christ Jesus" (Rom. 6:8–9, 11 NIV).

The message of Easter is that the way of being in Jesus, the way of living the new resurrected life is through participation. This message is very different than the message I all too frequently hear about Easter day. I hear that knowing God is accomplished through the way of intellectual evidence: Believe the facts and that will transform your life. I also hear that knowing God is accomplished through the way of emotion: Feel God. Feel forgiveness. Feel God in your heart. Certainly there is a place for evidence and feeling.

No one should deny the value of a good argument from Scripture for the resurrection nor should one negate the power of feeling the presence of the resurrected Christ in the songs sung, the sermon preached, and the Eucharist celebrated. But the emphasis of the early church fathers and the ancient church is knowing God through the way of participation. We participate in Christ by living the life of our baptism into his death and resurrection. This is a daily, existential, moment-by-moment experience as we choose in this or that situation to die to the sins for which Christ died and choose the life of the Spirit for which Christ was raised to a new life. St. Leo the Great, one of the fathers who carefully reflected on how our new life is identified with Christ's death and resurrection in the metaphor of baptism, had this to say:

> All that the Son of God did and taught for the reconciliation of the world is not simply known to us through the historical record of the past; we also experience it through the power of his present works. . . . It is not only the courageous, glorious martyrs who share in his suffering; all the faithful who are reborn also share it, and do so in the very act of their rebirth. For when men renounce Satan and believe in God, when they pass from corruption to a new life, when they lay aside the image of the earthly man and take on the form of the heavenly man, they go through a kind of death and resurrection. He who is received by Christ and receives Christ is not the same after his baptism as before; the body of the reborn Christian becomes the flesh of the crucified Christ.[4]

To summarize, Easter Sunday is the most important Sunday. It is the Sunday of all Sundays. It is the day of the new beginning of the entire cosmos, the day of resurrection.

In our worship we must be careful not to reduce our message to the Easter fact only. The Easter fact must include the message this fact proclaims: God makes all things new. It must also include the message that we have been raised with Christ. Calling God's people to die to sin and rise to the new life is central not only to Easter day but to the Easter season.

The Sundays of Easter

For those who have practiced Easter as a one-day event rather than a season, the thought of a season of seven weeks stretching to the day of Pentecost may be a challenge. However, once the themes of Easter and how they are related to the theme of conversion and union with Christ are seen, Easter as a season will be embraced with enthusiasm. But I must warn you, the themes of the Easter season run counter to our culture and the way we do church and spirituality today.

Recently I invited David Bunker, an artist, to address one of my worship classes at Northern Baptist Seminary on "the return to metaphor." I was struck by David's plea. "We live," he said, "in a day of metaphor. Our world is run by the images of consumerism, self-gratification, autonomy, the life of the rich and the famous, and so on. We have allowed these metaphors and images to shape our Christian experience and church. For Christianity to become healthy once again and to be what it is called to be, we need new metaphors."[5]

I agree! But there is no need to invent new metaphors (and David did not imply this). The original metaphors of the faith found in the New Testament and early church are old metaphors that need to be made new. The Easter season is the time to recapture some of these old metaphors and make them new and fresh. Finding, proclaiming, and living out these old metaphors in a new way will renew the church from its current cultural corruption and invigorate our spirituality. The primary metaphor for the Easter season is the church as the resurrected people living a resurrected spirituality. Because of Easter we are in union with Christ and are called to live in our baptismal identity in his resurrection.

This essential theme of Easter cannot be communicated in a day. It takes a season. And this season in the pattern of the Christian year is repeated yearly.

What are the themes of resurrection spirituality? Sundays two, three, and four deal with how resurrection spirituality is formed within the church in the life of its worship and under the personal care of the Good Shepherd. In Sundays five, six, and seven Jesus prepares the resurrected community for his ascension (forty days after Easter) and for the coming of the Spirit at Pentecost. (Pentecost falls on the eighth Sunday after Easter.) He especially gives his community the signs by which we will know that even though he has ascended to the Father, he is near and present to us as we remain in union with him.

These themes make for great worship through which God's community on earth continues to be formed by the ever-presence of the risen Lord.

Let us look at these themes and inquire of their significance for Christian formation.

Second Sunday of Easter: Church

It is highly appropriate that the second Sunday of Easter should focus on the church. The church is the community of God's people that is defined by the Easter event and called to live out the resurrected life.

The early church fathers were fond of making a comparison of the church with Israel. Israel was birthed and is defined by the exodus event. When Israel went astray the prophets called on the Israelites to repent of their ways and return to their origins in the exodus event. They were asked to remember their calling by living in the covenantal relationship established through the exodus deliverance.

The church has always been compared with Israel. Peter writes, "You are a chosen race, a royal priesthood, a holy nation, God's own people. . . . Once you were no people but now you are God's people; once you had not received mercy but now you have received mercy" (1 Peter 2:9–10).

Like Israel the church has frequently forgotten its origins. It passes through times of wilderness wanderings, times of apostasy, times when it forgets that it is the community of the death and resurrection of Jesus Christ—the community that is called to live out its resurrected spirituality. Could we be living in such a time?

Recently I spoke to a Bible church pastor who was inquiring about the Doctor of Ministry program at Northern Baptist Seminary. He was, in fact, interviewing me about our ministry emphasis as a way of determining whether our program of studies would speak to his pastoral concerns.

He asked, "What do you think is the major problem facing evangelical pastors?"

"I don't know that I could answer that question for sure," I said in a way, I suppose, of protecting myself. "I believe a major evangelical problem is to do evangelism in such a way that it leads to discipleship, then spiritual formation, and finally assimilation into the church. We evangelicals have done a good job of evangelizing people, but we haven't discipled, spiritually formed, and appropriately assimilated new converts into the church."

I don't know how he felt about my answer to his question. But he immediately said, "Let me tell you how I see my major problem. I spend most of my time trying to convince evangelicals to stay in the church. They are bored out of their minds and want to be Christians without the church."

His comment was not the first time I have heard someone speak of his or her discouragement with the church. Recently an eighty-four-year-old friend was describing his church to me, and as he shook his head he said, "Honestly, Bob, there are times I say to myself, 'What am I doing here?'" My friend is no spiritual slouch. He loves the church, the Word, and God's people, but he is in a church that though it is evangelical in name is full of dirty politics, is run by market- and business-driven principles, and follows a pattern of worship that borrows from TV talk shows and entertainment. He is so discouraged that he wonders how long he can tolerate a church shaped more by culture than by the biblical and early church principles of God's community. He is not the only one who thinks this way. Hardly a week goes by without someone sharing with me in person or by e-mail their distraught state and sense of confusion over the condition of the contemporary church. If you feel this way, then the second Sunday of the Easter season is a good time to address this problem and call the church to be the community of the resurrected people.

Easter is a time to call the church back to its roots, back to its original identity. Obviously we are aware that the original church was not perfect. The church has always struggled with its human dimension. Perhaps this is why the story of doubting Thomas is read on this Sunday. He wanted proof because his faith was based on evidence. The Enlightenment taught that only that which could be proven could be believed. We evangelicals have been greatly influenced by the modern demand for proof. It is as though faith is born by evidence. Yet the writer of Hebrews taught, "Now faith is being sure of what we hope for and certain of what we do not see" (Heb. 11:1 NIV).

The proof of the resurrection is not in rational argument but in the community of the resurrected people. The church is called to be a sign, a witness to the Easter message that Christ has overcome the powers of evil (Eph. 3:10). The church is called to be the embodied reality of a resurrected people who live out the reality of the resurrection. We gain an insight into this kind of community in Acts 2:42–47.

Some time ago I was in a Bible study in which the leader asked what I thought to be a provocative question. We read the Acts 2 account of the early church and he asked, "Is this account prescriptive or descriptive?" I recall a vigorous conversation, but I don't recall reaching an answer.

I have frequently gone back to that question and pondered what that early Christian community signified by its life. Luke's claim is that of a church that enjoyed strong worship, the experience of the miraculous, a sense of community, a vigorous home fellowship, glad and generous hearts, the goodwill of the people, and conversion growth. I am still not sure if this account is prescriptive or descriptive, but either way, it speaks volumes to the current condition of many churches.

The point to take into account is what the life of the church signifies. It speaks; it communicates. Today many feel that the current church signifies the culture. We have dumbed down the church, making it so palatable that it has no edge. We need to take the church back to its origins, to its roots in the death and resurrection of Jesus Christ, and once again become a community of the resurrection.

This ancient Jerusalem church was a church that signified resurrection spirituality. They lived the resurrected life. Today the real key to church renewal is not strategy, as we have been told by church growth movements, but like the early church, we are to embody the resurrection. Those communities that become corporate expressions of resurrection spirituality are the communities that will attract and keep the unsaved and unchurched. People are not held in the church through gimmicks, entertainment, or even so-called relevance. What will renew the church today is the communal experience of the resurrection. The church is the context in which that resurrection experience is named and known.

Third Sunday of Easter: Worship

Worship is the constant celebration of the Easter event. It is in worship that resurrection spirituality is learned and experienced.

Has the church fallen into a wilderness wandering in its worship? I know of at least two quagmires: worship that is constantly explained and worship that encourages a romantic relationship with God.

I have been in many communities in which worship is constantly explained. Once again, it is the impact of the Enlightenment. The only aspect of humanity that is capable of perception, it is argued, is the mind. So everything done in worship is verbalized. "We are going to do such and such. Now that we have done that, we are going to do this. Do you see and understand the connection?" We verbalize confessions, explain hymns, and, worst of all, beat the Lord's Supper to death with explanation on top of explanation. No wonder people are bored. We need to learn the biblical action of worship and trust the symbols we do to be performative. Worship is a symbolization whereby we proclaim (yes, words are used), sing (no explanation needed), and enact (yes, dramatize) the original event that forms and shapes us into the pattern of his death and resurrection.

Then there is worship in which a relationship with God is romanticized. Ultimately romantic worship can be traced back to the impact of the romantic movement of the nineteenth century. Here a relationship with God is expressed in emotional and sentimental terms often using romantic images. Some contemporary songs are overly romantic. I attended a new church recently in which God was romanced in the music. A couple in front of me acted out the entire scenario. As love songs were sung they embraced, looked longingly into each other's eyes, and even kissed. Worship is not a romantic experience with God even though it may be very moving and touch the heart deeply. Worship does result in great joy because it proclaims the power of Christ to raise us from our dislocations in life to a relocation in God.

A favorite reading for the third Sunday of Easter is the powerful account of Cleopas and his companion on the road to Emmaus (Luke 24). This story is vital for the renewal of our worship because it is all about how to structure worship out of the death and resurrection and how to experience resurrection spirituality in worship.

Today's worship seems to have no internal rhythm, no discernable pattern of spiritual formation, no sense of internal flow. Liturgical scholarship finds in the Emmaus story the shape of early Christian worship. It is a fourfold pattern; note the structure. Cleopis and his companion are on the road. Jesus walks with them and proclaims the meaning of his death and resurrection. Next, they are at the table with Jesus. In the breaking of the bread he is known to them. They then run back to Jerusalem to witness to the disciples in the upper room: He is risen for we knew him in the breaking of the bread! Worship is based on this structure. Here it is in its most simple yet profound form:

> We gather
> To hear the good news
> To break bread together
> To go forth and tell others

Inside this fourfold pattern is the content of the death and resurrection and the message of hope. Note that this worship is God's doing. Jesus initiates the relationship on the road. Jesus proclaims his death and resurrection. Jesus encounters them at the breaking of the bread. Jesus shows up in their telling of others. The Bible is clear: It is always God who initiates a relationship. What is true generally is also true in worship. Worship is God's work.

The Greek word *liturgeia*, from which we derive our word *liturgy*, means "the work of the people." Our work in worship is to do the work of remembrance and hope. In worship we remember God's acts of salvation in history, especially God's work in the death and resurrection of Jesus to be a sacrifice for our sins and to be a victor over the powers of evil. Therefore in worship we anticipate his coming again, the total destruction of evil, and the reign of God's shalom over the entire created world.

So worship signifies God and God's mission to rescue creatures and creation. But note what this kind of worship does. It is performative. That is, it does something for those who do the work of proclaiming and enacting God's work. It transforms them.

Cleopas and his companion were dislocated as they walked the road to Emmaus. Jesus met them in their point of need, proclaimed the meaning for them of his death and resurrection, and encountered them through a transforming experience at the table. They were changed people when they ran back to Jerusalem to proclaim the resurrection.

True worship is not a program, not a romantic feeling about God, but the communication of a real and genuine transformation of a person's life and outlook.

Every Sunday is a "little Easter." Every Sunday of the year is a celebration of the Easter event. The work of the people in "doing the Christ event" through memory and hope is the source for personal and corporate formation into resurrection spirituality. And this is the message of the third Sunday of Easter.

Fourth Sunday of Easter: The Good Shepherd

I was in New York City on the fourth Sunday of Easter in the year that I was writing this book. My wife and I chose to visit St. Bartholomew Church in Manhattan. The Gospel lesson and the sermon was on Jesus and the Good Shepherd (John 10:1–21). The guest speaker, a woman bishop, began her sermon by saying that she was at a disadvantage because she had never actually met a real live shepherd nor did she know much about shepherding. But, she said, she turned to books and articles written by or about shepherding in order to understand the text better.

My first impression was, "Good for you!" I have grown weary and quite skeptical of the recent notion of finding a dynamic equivalent for those biblical metaphors we do not experience in our own culture. I was relieved she wasn't going to reinterpret this Scripture through some metaphor that was common to us all. I did not want to hear about the good mechanic or the good teacher or the good tour guide. I wanted to hear about the Good Shepherd.

Cultural equivalence has frequently resulted in a dumbing down or in a downright perverted sense of Scripture. I am in agreement with Stanley Hauerwas, who insists that in a postmodern world we must return to a countercultural view of Christianity. An essential ingredient of this countercultural faith is to understand the language of faith. This is exactly what this bishop did. She taught us the language and grammar of being a shepherd, and my eyes were opened. I don't remember the whole sermon, but several insights made an impression on me.

First, a shepherd is utterly committed to his flock. He lives with them and dwells with them day and night. He knows each of the sheep. He knows their moods, their needs, their likes, and their dislikes. Sheep are not like cows that need to be driven or forced, so a good shepherd leads the sheep, he never drives them. Appropriately, the psalm appointed for this Sunday is Psalm 23. "The LORD is my shepherd, I shall not want. He makes me lie down in green pastures; he leads me beside still waters; he restores my soul. He leads me in right paths for his name's sake" (vv. 1–3 NRSV).

The image of the good shepherd, the shepherd who will give his life for his sheep, is that of servant leadership. Jesus the Good Shepherd has given his life for us, his sheep. And having been raised from death, he now leads us on into green pastures.

This brings us to the second major point made by the bishop. The sheep will follow no other shepherd. They know the voice of the shepherd, his scent, and the touch of his hand. Another shepherd may come among the flock, may call out to the sheep, and may follow all of the ritual of the genuine shepherd, but the sheep will not budge. They stand or lie as though nothing is happening. But the moment the true shepherd speaks, they obey his command because they know him and trust him.

It is compelling that Psalm 23 was read at baptisms in the ancient church. Baptism, as I have mentioned above, is a baptism into Jesus. We are called in baptism to identify with the Good Shepherd who laid down his life for us. We are called to follow him in the pattern of death and resurrection. The fourth Sunday of Easter reminds us that we have a leader, the Good Shepherd whose voice we are to hear, whose life we are to follow.

Fifth Sunday of Easter: Ministry in the Church

Beginning with the fifth Sunday of Easter, there is a decided shift in the Easter emphasis. We know the time between the resurrection and the ascension was a time of teaching. Luke informs us that Jesus appeared to his disciples "during forty days . . . speaking about the kingdom of God" (Acts 1:3 NRSV). It is generally conceded that his teaching about his death and resurrection, the meaning of it, and the meaning of the kingdom are contained in the Gospels and Epistles.

Here is the shift. Jesus knew that he had to prepare his disciples for his ascension and return to the Father. He had to address the question of how he would continue to remain present with them and guide them in his physical absence. The focus for the rest of the Easter season is on this issue. Jesus prepares his disciples to be the church, his body, the continued presence of Jesus in the world. The church is itself a *sign* of Jesus and, as we will see, contains additional signs of the presence of the resurrected and now ascended Lord.

The fifth Sunday of Easter focuses on the sign of ministry. Jesus taught his disciples that "the Son of man came not to be served but to serve, and to give his life as a ransom for many" (Matt. 20:28). Now the disciples and soon the church had to learn how to become ministers of the people, following the example of their Good Shepherd.

This theme, the continued incarnational presence of the ascended Lord through the church, emphasizes the need for the church to experience the presence of Jesus by loving each other as Christ loved the church and gave his life for it (John 13:31–35).

I think we have forgotten that the church is called to be Jesus to the world. In the latter part of the twentieth century the church began to identify itself with corporate America. You know the scenario—a market-driven, business-model church, it was argued, would use resources more efficiently and produce more converts. The kingdom will be built by the Wal-Mart church with something for everybody, spiritual goods marketed to the spiritual consumer, and a managerial staff sensitive to strategy.

This culture-driven model of the church does not seem to square with the teachings of Jesus. Recently I attended a lecture by Glen Wagner, the author of *Beyond Church Inc.* and pastor of Calvary Church in Charlotte, North Carolina. In a personal conversation he said, "Bob, I have been there. I have done the megachurch thing. But I couldn't stay there. Now I am trying to teach a church burned by megachurch principles the way of Jesus. It is no easy task. It requires a whole paradigm shift."

The paradigm shift is to recover resurrection spirituality in ministry. All who are in Christ are ministers. Christ is the chief minister, and through ordination Christ has appointed some in his flock to lead the way and be shepherds in his name. Shepherding never exercises power. The true shepherd is the one who bears the mark of the ultimate Shepherd. The chief ministers in the church are called to lead us by example—bearing fruit and above all leading through love.

Sixth Sunday of Easter: The Spirit

In the sixth Sunday of Easter we are coming very close to the time of the ascension. Ascension Day occurs on the Thursday between the sixth and seventh Sundays of Easter. Some churches will celebrate the ascension on one of these Sundays.

It is during this time period that Jesus prepares his disciples in a more intense way and tells them more about the coming of the Holy Spirit and his ministry in the church. In John 14 Philip asks, "Lord, show us the Father," to which Jesus replies, "Whoever has seen me has seen the Father" (vv. 8–9 NRSV). Jesus then carries this insight on his union with the Father to affirm that he is sending the Spirit who "will be in you" (v. 17 NRSV). He is teaching that those who are in union with the Holy Spirit are in union with him and through him in union with the Father. Here Jesus clearly teaches the theology of resurrection spirituality. The early church fathers, especially those of the Eastern tradition, developed the theology of union with the Triune God through the gift of the Holy Spirit. They believed the empowerment of the Holy Spirit was connected to the visible and tangible signs of baptism and Eucharist.

In the modern world of evangelicalism there is a tendency to disassociate the Spirit from signs. But in the early church the sign of baptism was accompanied by the sealing of the Spirit: "In him you also, when you had heard the word of truth, the gospel of your salvation, and had believed in him, were marked with the seal of the promised Holy Spirit; this is the pledge of our inheritance toward redemption as God's own people, to the praise of his glory" (Eph. 1:13–14 NRSV). In baptism and the faith it represents, one receives the Holy Spirit.

The early church fathers also associated the Holy Spirit with the Eucharist. In the ancient eucharistic prayer recorded by Hippolytus in *The Apostolic Tradition* and written at the turn of the third century, Hippolytus records for us the common triune prayer said at the bread and wine. After praising the Father and remembering the saving work of the Son, the prayer to the Holy Spirit calls upon the Spirit to gather the church into one and then to confirm our faith in truth. The bread and wine received in the community of Christ's body communicates the truth about Jesus Christ. It also communicates the union we have through the Spirit with the Son and through him with the Father.

The early church fathers saw "relationship" written in large letters over *baptism* and *the Eucharist*. For example, it was common among the fathers to interpret the Old Testament through a typological exegesis. They saw the intimacy of the Song of Solomon finding fulfillment in baptism and the Eucharist. Baptism is our marriage while Eucharist is the kiss of love.

In our modern, rationalistic world we tend to see baptism and Eucharist as *our* signs of devotion to God. But in the ancient church baptism was first God's sign of our union with him and then our sign of embracing this union and its calling to live in the pattern of death and resurrection. Eucharist is also God's sign—a kind of affirmation of Jesus' death for us and his resurrection for us. Again, the Spirit confirms the truth of Jesus' death and resurrection in which we were baptized and through bread and wine continually nourishes us in the pattern of death and resurrection spirituality first confirmed at our baptism.

The Spirit, who comforts us and leads us into all truth, is associated with signs—the church, ministry, love, baptism, Eucharist, and more. All these signs focus on what is central to our faith, the source of our spiritual lives: Jesus Christ and his death and resurrection for us. These signs not only remind us of our union with him, when taken in faith they convey our relationship.

Seventh Sunday of Easter: The Prayer of Jesus

On the Sunday before Pentecost it is fitting that the church remember the final prayer of Jesus in the Garden of Gethsemane (John 17). The focus of the prayer is on God's glory, the glory that the Son shares with the Father, and the glory now shared by those who are in the Son.

God's glory is always associated with his mighty acts of salvation. His glory was particularly manifested in the exodus event and the calling of Israel to be his people. God's glory is manifest at the baptism of Jesus, at the transfiguration, and in his death and resurrection, and it will be manifested at his return to destroy the powers of evil and to reign eternally over all creation. We also know that the glory of God is manifested in his ascension. He has returned to the glory he has always had with the Father before the creation of the world.

Most stunning for us is that Jesus sees that his glory is to be continued through his people. "The glory that you have given me I have given them, so that they may be one, as we are one" (John 17:22 NRSV). It is an astounding fact that the great glory of the Son with the Father and the glory of God's mighty acts of salvation is a glory given to the church so that through its oneness the glory of God may be made known in all the earth.

Here is yet another sign of resurrection spirituality: the oneness of the church. This does not mean that we can't recognize the diversity of the church, but it does speak to our prejudices and our failure to affirm the essential oneness of the church. There was a time when I would insist that the only basis for the unity of the church was truth. By that I meant my brand of truth. The *true truth*, to borrow a phrase from Francis Schaeffer, is our unity in the person of Jesus Christ—God who became man to restore fallen creatures and creation. Some may consider this affirmation a reduction and insist on conformity to a whole system of theological thought—maybe romanticism or Eastern Orthodoxy or Reformed or Lutheran or Anabaptist or Wesleyan theology. These are traditions about the tradition, which is Jesus Christ. I have learned that an absolute affirmation of the uniqueness of Christ and of his death and resurrection for creatures and creation presses me to understand and appreciate all the traditions. We are a community of communities. We may have our differences, but they are slight by comparison to what we hold in common.

To summarize, the Easter season is all about our resurrection spirituality. Our calling is to live in the pattern of his death and resurrection. To encourage us in this calling God has given us the church, the Holy Spirit, and the signs of our union with him—baptism, Eucharist, servant ministry, love, and unity.[6]

Two Celebrations

The two primary celebrations of salvation history in the Easter season are Ascension Day and Pentecost Sunday.

Ascension Day

I am of the opinion that Ascension Day comes and goes without any notice in most of our churches. This is a great pity because the ascension figures prominently in God's plan of salvation. The ascension occurs forty days after Easter. During those forty days our Lord has been teaching his disciples and getting them ready for his departure and the coming of the Holy Spirit (Acts 1:1–11). Ascension Day now falls on a Thursday, ten days before the day of Pentecost, but it is appropriate to celebrate the ascension on the Sunday before Pentecost as well.

What do we celebrate on Ascension Day? The interpretation of ascension is scattered in references here and there in the Epistles, but the two most prominent theological interpretations are found in Ephesians and Hebrews. The writer of Hebrews has a profound understanding of the work of Jesus Christ as our High Priest. In chapters 8–10 he compares the work of the high priest in the Old Testament tabernacle with the work of Jesus. The Old Testament high priest entered into the holy of holies once a year to offer sacrifices "for himself and for the sins [of] the people" (Heb. 9:7 NIV). This sacrifice served as a "copy and shadow of what is in heaven" (Heb. 8:5 NIV). But Christ, who is the true and eternal High Priest, "did not enter [the Most Holy Place] by means of the blood of goats and calves; but he entered the Most Holy Place once for all by his own blood, having obtained eternal redemption" (Heb. 9:12 NIV).

When the writer compares the work of Christ to that of the Old Testament high priest, he calls it "the greater and more perfect tabernacle" (Heb. 9:11 NIV). It is the "superior" covenant that is "founded on better promises" (Heb. 8:6 NIV). It is a "new" covenant that has made the former covenant "obsolete" (Heb. 8:13). It is a better covenant because Jesus has now "appeared once for all at the end of the ages to do away with sin by the sacrifice of himself" (Heb. 9:26 NIV). While this typological interpretation of Jesus is a profound insight into the work of Jesus as a sacrifice for sin, the writer does not stop with the earthly work of Jesus.

Jesus ascends in order to continue his work as our eternal intercessor. The Hebrews writer proclaims, "Now there have been many of those priests, since death prevented them from continuing in office; but Jesus lives forever, he has a permanent priesthood. Therefore he is able to save completely those who come to God through him, because he always lives to intercede for them" (Heb. 7:23–25 NIV).

The work of Christ on our behalf is eternal. "The point of what we are saying is this: We do have such a high priest, who sat down at the right hand of the throne of the Majesty in heaven, and who serves in the sanctuary, the true tabernacle set up by the Lord, not by man" (Heb. 8:1–2 NIV). Jesus Christ, this man who is God, participated in our humanity to die for us and to be resurrected for us, and he now has ascended to the very throne of God to continually represent us to the Father. For "he entered heaven itself, now to appear for us in God's presence" (Heb. 9:24 NIV). *He who did everything that ever needed to be done to save us now continually stands before the Father interceding for us!*

In his letter to the Ephesian community Paul provides us with another breathtaking insight only known because of the ascension: Christ's ascension is the hope to which we have been called. "I pray also that the eyes of your heart may be enlightened in order that you may know the hope to which he has called you, the riches of his glorious inheritance in the saints" (Eph. 1:18 NIV).

The early church fathers saw the ascension of the Lord as the lifting up of the human nature of Jesus to the throne of God. The eternal Word was united to a perfect human nature in Jesus. Because Jesus participated in our human nature (without sin) and because through faith we are united with Jesus, our human but redeemed nature, united with Jesus, is lifted to the very throne of God. Leo the Great, an early church father, puts this profound truth this way: "For on this day not only have we been confirmed in our possession of paradise, but we have entered heaven in the person of Christ; through his ineffable grace we have regained far more than we had lost through the devil's hatred."[7]

Paul also calls our attention to one more theological aspect of the ascension. In his ascended state our Lord has been seated "far above all rule and authority, power and dominion, and every title that can be given, not only in the present age but also in the one to come. And God

. . . appointed him to be head over everything for the church, which is his body, the fullness of him who fills everything in every way" (Eph. 1:21–23 NIV).

The truth that Jesus is "above all rule and authority" and "head over everything for the church" points to the very purpose of the church in the world: "His intent was that now, through the church, the manifold wisdom of God should be made known to the rulers and authorities in the heavenly realms" (Eph. 3:10 NIV).

But one question remains: If Jesus has ascended into heaven, has he left any signs of his presence among us? Clearly the foremost answer to this question is the sending of the Holy Spirit, which the church will experience at Pentecost. Jesus connected his ascension with the coming of the Spirit. He told his disciples that "'you will receive power when the Holy Spirit comes on you; and you will be my witnesses in Jerusalem, and in all Judea and Samaria, and to the ends of the earth.' After he said this, he was taken up before their very eyes" (Acts 1:8–9 NIV). The working of the Spirit is the sign of the ascended Lord's presence.

What signs of the Holy Spirit do we have among us? Certainly the church, which is the body of Christ, signifies the presence of the ascended Lord. And the church recognizes that his presence is made known in the assembled people. For "where two or three are gathered in my name, there am I in the midst of them" (Matt. 18:20). The communal experience of the church is that the presence of Christ is made known in the special signs given to the church by Jesus—the signs of water and of bread and wine. For in the waters of baptism we are identified with Jesus in his death and resurrection (Rom. 6:1–11), and in receiving the bread and wine we partake of his presence (John 6).

This past spring I was asked to lead an ascension service in chapel at Northern Baptist Seminary. It was a simple, thirty-minute service so I did nothing elaborate—only the essentials of ascension. Since ascension is a festal occasion, we began with a processional hymn, "Hail Thee Festival Day." As we sang this glorious and exuberant hymn of Christ's entrance into his glory, my administrative assistant, Ashley Olsen, danced, expressing the joy of Jesus' entrance into heaven with movement.

After the opening prayer, Scriptures of the ascension were read and I gave a brief sermon pointing to the theological interpretation of the ascension given by Paul and the writer of Hebrews. Then I asked, "Has Jesus left us without any signs of his presence among us?" I answered with a resounding "No" and pointed to the church and to the water of baptism and to the bread and wine as signs of his ongoing presence among us.

I then pointed to the bowl of water on the table, and taking a handful of water and raising it, I let it splash back into the bowl and then spoke of how water is a sign of Jesus' presence. As we sang "He Is Lord," confessing the ascended status of Jesus, I invited all who were there to come, take some water, and make the sign of the cross to signify his presence. They could then wear the invisible tattoo of the cross on their foreheads and in their hearts as a sign of his abiding presence in their lives. I wasn't sure how this would be received since this is a Baptist seminary. However, all came and all signed the cross on their foreheads.

In the modern world we evangelicals tended to see symbols as dead and empty. But now, in the new world of postmodernity, a new sensitivity to the performative power of symbol has emerged. Whereas the Christian leadership of the boomer era called for a worship without symbols, the younger evangelicals are restoring crosses to their worship space and recovering the use of water, oil, bread, and wine not as "just symbols" but as powerful ways to proclaim and enact the gospel.

Perhaps in the next Easter season you will be led to conduct (or to attend) a service of ascension. It is, as I have shown from the Scripture, an important event in the history of God's salvation. It is not a season but an event. If we wish to form congregational and personal spirituality, we will call attention to the ascended Lord who eternally intercedes for us and is always with us through the church and the signs of our identity with him (water) and of his continual nourishment (bread and wine).[8]

Pentecost

Pentecost plays a crucial role in salvation history. Yet there are many communities that claim to be Gospel oriented who do not celebrate Pentecost. In order to bring God's people into a full experience of the Good News, an emphasis on Pentecost is necessary. Broadly speaking, Pentecost brings understanding to the followers of Jesus, empowers them in ministry, establishes the church, and points to the end of history when the kingdom of Christ will be established over all the earth.

First, Pentecost results in a clearer and deeper understanding of Jesus. Throughout his ministry Jesus taught his disciples the purpose of his presence on earth, referring in particular to his divine origin and his destiny in death and resurrection. Obviously these comments were veiled as his closest disciples failed to get it. During the forty days after his resurrection he also "spoke about the kingdom of God" (Acts 1:3 NIV). Again, while the teaching may have been intense, greater clarity was achieved through the coming of the Holy Spirit. For by the insight of the Spirit, Peter declared that Jesus was the fulfillment of all the messianic hopes and was Lord. Here, in Acts 2:36, is the heart of the *kerygma:* "Therefore let all Israel be assured of this: God has made this Jesus, whom you crucified, both Lord and Christ" (NIV).

This proclamation must have been clearly understood, for it was met with the dramatic question, "Brothers, what shall we do?" to which Peter replied, "Repent and be baptized, every one of you, in the name of Jesus Christ for the forgiveness of your sins. And you will receive the gift of the Holy Spirit" (Acts 2:37–38 NIV). While this was a *start* in understanding the faith, it was a crucial start. As we now know, the Spirit continued to pour out an understanding of the faith as recorded in the New Testament literature.

Second, the coming of the Holy Spirit resulted in a new empowerment. It was here that the mission of the church given by Jesus just before his ascension began to take form. Present at the feast of Pentecost were "God-fearing Jews from every nation under heaven" (Acts 2:5 NIV). Shortly thereafter the message of God's mission in Jesus Christ was proclaimed in the known world. The Spirit also provided gifts to God's people. The gift of tongues was given to proclaim God's message throughout the world—and as we follow the missionary journeys and the spread of the faith in the first century, other gifts of the Spirit unfold. One of these gifts is that the Spirit prays prayers for us that we are not able to utter (Rom. 8:27).

A third result of Pentecost is the church. Christians have always marked Pentecost Sunday as the birthday of the church. The church is, by the power of the Holy Spirit, the continuation of the presence of Jesus in and to the world. The metaphor of "the body of Christ" that became common in the early church captures this incarnational dimension of the church. While Christ is seated at the right hand of the Father, he is also completely present in a mystical way to his body, the church.

Finally, Pentecost points to the end of the world and to the establishment of God's kingdom over all that God has created. Peter proclaims that Pentecost begins "the last days" and points to "the coming of the great and glorious day of the Lord" (Acts 2:17, 20; see vv. 17–21). This quote from Joel (3:1–5) emphasizes the judgment that is to come, a judgment that is clarified in the later Epistles as the final blow to the powers of evil, which will be followed by the establishment of God's kingdom over all (see 2 Peter 3:10–14).

We now live in the final days, the time between the coming of the Holy Spirit, and the return of our Lord. Therefore, Pentecost is an essential moment in God's saving time, the moment in which we now live, awaiting the return of our Lord.

How to Celebrate Pentecost

The theological insights I have summarized above shape Pentecost worship—its environment, its song, its Scripture reading and preaching, its practice of baptism, its consecration of evangelists, and its Eucharist. My assistant, the liturgical dancer mentioned earlier, was invited to dance at a Pentecost celebration in a Baptist church. She told me excitedly about the environment—red, the color of Pentecost, was everywhere. Red clothing was worn by worshipers, there were red banners as well as red pulpit and communion cloths. A red stole was worn by the pastor. Red cloth was draped over the pews. Red flags were twirled by the dancers.

How significant. We remember what we see. Here was truth in color. Color in motion. Color proclaiming. Color acting. Color reminding. Color being performative—speaking, delivering, communicating the truth that the Holy Spirit has come. Most of us will forget almost everything else done in a service like that. But the significance of red as the sign of the Spirit who has come will remain and call us to the meaning of the Spirit in our lives and in the life of the church.[9]

Conclusion

The Pentecost service ends one season in the Christian year and begins another. Pentecost Sunday ends the extraordinary season that began on the first Sunday of Advent. In approximately six months the church has been carried through all the saving events of God—his incarnation, manifestation to the world, life, death, resurrection, and ascension as well as the coming of the Holy Spirit. All these crucial events form faith and the spiritual life.

Obviously these days can be observed in a mere ritualistic manner that does not result in faith and Christian formation. However, ministers and congregations that focus on the Good News of Christ and salvation and do so with passion will communicate in a spiritually forming way the central truths of the Christian faith. In a clear, directed, and evangelical practice of the Christian year, there is no missing of the point.

Worship now moves into another season—ordinary time. Here the church calls to mind the teaching of the church and the practices of the Christian life as recorded in the New Testament writings.

Table 8: A Summary of Easter Spirituality

Theme	Spiritual Emphasis
Why is white the color of Easter?	White is the color of Easter because it is the color of new, clean, and set apart. White represents festivity.
What is the spirituality of Easter?	The resurrection happened not only in a particular time and place, it is also to happen within me.

Continued

Explain the historic meaning of the resurrection message.	The resurrection message is that Christ has won a victory over the powers of evil; he is Lord of all creatures and creation. Christians see the Lord through Easter eyes.
Explain the personal, existential meaning of resurrection spirituality.	In resurrection spirituality we are called to live in the pattern of death to sin and resurrection to new life.
What is the corporate meaning of resurrection spirituality?	The origins of the church are in the Easter event. When the corporate church lives the resurrection life, it acts as a witness to truth. Worship is the continual remembrance of the meaning of the Christ event for the whole world. Jesus is the Good Shepherd over the church. All who minister in the church do so in the name of Jesus. The presence of the Holy Spirit in the church is communicated in the signs of the assembly at baptism and Eucharist. The glory of God continues through the church.
What is the spirituality of the ascension?	Jesus, who died and was resurrected for us and our salvation, now eternally intercedes on our behalf before the Father.
What is the spirituality of Pentecost?	At Pentecost the Holy Spirit comes to continually enrich our understanding of Jesus and to empower our ministry in his name.

A Prayer for Easter

Almighty God, whom truly to know is everlasting life: Grant us so perfectly to know your Son Jesus Christ to be the way, the truth, and the life, that we may steadfastly follow his steps in the way that leads to eternal life; through Jesus Christ your Son our Lord, who lives and reigns with you, in the unity of the Holy Spirit, one God, forever and ever, Amen.

From *The Book of Common Prayer*

Questions for Reflection

1. Describe Easter spirituality in your own words.
2. Reflect on the Easter message that God's salvation extends to the whole world and covers the face of the earth.
3. How is the church the sign in the world of the salvation of the world?
4. Is the worship of your church a continual celebration of the death and resurrection of Christ? How so?
5. What does it mean for you that Christ is your eternal intercessor?
6. How has the Spirit brought empowerment to your life and ministry?

Resources for Easter Worship and Preaching

See Robert Webber, ed., *The Services of the Christian Year*, vol. 5 of *The Complete Library of Christian Worship* (Peabody, MA: Hendrickson, 1994), 373–426.

- Introduction to Easter worship
- Resources for worship during the season of Easter
- Resources for the arts in worship

8

AFTER PENTECOST

A *Time to Experience God's Renewing Presence*

We who have once for all cloned ourselves in Christ, and been made worthy to have him dwelling within us, may show everyone, if we choose, simply by the strict discipline of our life and without saying a word, the power of him who dwells in us.

John Chrysostom (AD 347–407)

The period between Pentecost and the beginning of Advent is called *ordinary time*. By contrast the period through Advent, Christmas, Epiphany, Lent, the Great Triduum, and the Easter season ending on Pentecost Sunday is called *extraordinary time*. Extraordinary time is so designated because its chief purpose is to celebrate the specific historic, supernatural acts of God in history that result in the salvation of creatures and creation. Most of this book is about this extraordinary time and how special attention to the great saving events of God form congregational and personal spirituality.

Does that mean that ordinary time is a lesser time and not spiritually formative? Not at all. The word *ordinary* is a useful word for the period after Pentecost, but it is not entirely accurate. The word *ordinary* is used in our Christian-year vocabulary because it serves the special nature of extraordinary time by way of contrast. But ordinary time is anything but ordinary. Let me explain.

The Nature of Ordinary Time

The emphasis of ordinary time (the period from Pentecost to Advent) is on Sunday after Sunday worship. In order to understand how *non-ordinary* ordinary time is, it is necessary to review why the church worships on Sunday. We must begin with the Jewish Shabbat.

Shabbat

A few years ago I became friends with an orthodox rabbi. On one occasion he invited my wife and me and another couple to a Friday night Shabbat meal at his home. Upon arrival his wife pointed to eight candles burning in a holder in the dining room. "Those candles," she said, "are lighted in honor of the four people in our family and the four of you who share Shabbat with us this evening." This symbol of the burning candles was a beautiful act of hospitality and made us feel at home immediately.

We first spent some time looking at antiques, hearing the stories attached to them, and generally getting acquainted. During this time the rabbi casually said to me, "We Jews just love the Shabbat. It is a time for rest and relationship with those we love. We don't do any work. We don't answer the phone, cook, or even close doors. We just rest and relate."

"Oh," I thought, "to be a Jew."

Soon we gathered around the table. The rabbi first broke a loaf of bread and then, thanking God for the gifts of the earth, passed it around asking each of us to eat a piece of the broken bread. Then lifting a bottle of wine he poured the wine into a cup praying the ancient Jewish prayer of thanks to God for the gift of the vine. The poured wine was passed around the table and we each drank of it. Then we ate. It was delicious food. And the conversation that focused on our families and our faith was rich with meaning.

At the end of the meal the rabbi explained that in the Jewish tradition it was common to pray at the close of the meal as well. He said, "My wife and I will sing a psalm to each other in Hebrew. You may not understand the words, so just enter the spirit of our prayer." The rabbi, who also happens to be a professional musician, began to sing, and his wife, in a beautiful voice, sang the refrain as they made their way through the psalm. When the song finished, the rabbi looked across the table into the eyes of his wife and praised her. "I thank God for giving you to be my wife," he said. "My life is blessed by you and my cup runs over. You are a good woman, a great mother to our children, and a gracious hostess to our guests. May God give us many years together."

Then calling his children to his side, he laid his hands on their heads, one by one, and spoke a blessing upon them. They ran off to play and we soon got into our car to return home. As we were driving home we talked of the pleasant time we had, of the hospitality, of the love in the family. And we especially commented on the commitment to rest.

The key to the Jewish Shabbat is rest. This, as we all know, derives from the days of creation and the rest God entered on the seventh day. The Jewish tradition of resting from sundown Friday to sundown Saturday is the day of *Shabbat*, the day that all creation is at rest.

Sunday

So why Sunday worship? In the Jewish reckoning of time, Saturday is the seventh day of the week, making Sunday the first day of the week. The resurrection of Jesus occurred on Sunday, the first day of the week. The Gospel writers all carefully document the resurrection on the first day of the week (Matt. 28:1; Mark 16:2; Luke 24:1; John 20:1, 19). The most important day of the week for Christians is Sunday. Why? Sunday was called "the Lord's day" (Rev. 1:10). As Saturday is the special day for Jews, so Sunday is the special day for Christians. Sunday is the day of resurrection, the day of the new creation, the day of the beginning again.

On the seventh day God rested from his work of creation. But on the first day God acted to re-create the world. Thus Sunday, the eighth day, brings creation and re-creation together in a very special event—Sunday worship. Thus the Sundays of ordinary time are not so ordinary—they celebrate the full story of God's action in history to save creatures and creation. This is the special nature of ordinary time. It is the day to celebrate the re-creation of the world.

The Special Nature of Sunday

I am of the personal opinion that the true meaning of Sunday worship has been lost in many of our churches. In some communities Sunday is the day of revival, the day for the seeker, or the day to teach. Historically Sunday is the day of God's re-creation, the day that promises that God will renew the face of the earth. Historically Sunday worship expresses three truths: It remembers God's saving action in history; it experiences God's renewing presence; and it anticipates the consummation of God's work in the new heavens and the new earth.

Sunday Remembers God's Saving Action in History

Sunday worship expresses Christian truth through remembrance of the God who acts. Recently in one of my worship classes at Northern Baptist Seminary I was giving a lecture on worship hermeneutic. The class was made up of people from a number of different denominations and cultures. My point was that to know why you worship and how you worship you must understand the hermeneutic (method of interpretation) that has shaped your tradition.

I spoke of the hermeneutic that makes the revelation of God in the Bible the starting point of worship. This hermeneutic sees worship as teaching. Thus worship is primarily preaching. It reminds me of an instance during my seminary days when I was interim pastor of a small church. A guest preacher said, "Bob, you better shorten the preliminaries today, I've got a long sermon." His view of worship was that the main event was the sermon. I actually know of people in this tradition who come late to Sunday worship because "the sermon is the only thing that matters anyway."

If your hermeneutic is the church, as in the medieval tradition, then your starting point for worship is the institution of the church doing worship according to the established rubrics. God is communicated in a mystical way through the sacraments of the church in worship.

In many current churches the hermeneutic of worship is primarily self-generated. *I* worship God. *I* proclaim God's worth. *I* worship and honor him. A good friend of mine has been thinking seriously about worship, and he recently raised a question about the theology of a worship song. He loved the tune and wanted to sing it, but he had some ambivalence about using it in a forthcoming worship. "Bob," he said, "I'm thinking about using this song that proclaims 'We enthrone you,' but I am not sure. What do you think?" My immediate question was, "Do we enthrone Christ, or has the Father enthroned him?"

The point is that this highly experiential worship that arises from the self is not true biblical worship. It makes the false assumption that *I* have the capacity to offer worship. It assumes that *I* give worship to God. I've been in many worshiping communities where that assumption is made. I know that I have nothing to offer God. I can no longer sing those songs that ask me to go deep inside of myself and from within myself offer God praise. I am worn out by the self-effort. Attempts on my part to proclaim God's worth seem hollow and empty, even legalistic and phony.

Students listened as I explicated these hermeneutics. I am not completely sure what they were thinking, but after explaining these and other hermeneutics, I said, "Let me give you one more." Addressing the African-American students in the class, I said, "I think your hermeneutic arises from the exodus event. You identify with the Hebrews who were enslaved. You identify with their deliverance from enslavement, their redemption, their new beginning." I was taken aback by the response of the African-American students as they shouted, "That's it!" "Yes!" "Come on now!" "Preach it!" "Praise God!" and "Say it again!"

In this description I not only touched on what black worship does intuitively, I touched on the true biblical hermeneutic of worship—remembrance. In worship we remember God's mighty acts of salvation. The exodus event is a type of the Christ event. God finds us in our state of slavery to sin, to the rulers of the air, and to the powers and principalities of this world. God's mission is to rescue us. Worship does God's mission. It proclaims and enacts it; it sings it, teaches it, and shapes us into the people of God's saving event in Jesus Christ.

Let me give you an example. Some time ago a good friend, an Episcopal priest, asked me to take him to a Bible church. "I've never been to a Bible church," he said. "I'd like to worship in that tradition." So I took him to a Sunday evening service at the Wheaton Bible Church. The service began with a few songs. Then the minister said, "Let us pray." And he prayed:

> Lord we give you thanks for creating us in your image.
> When we fell away into sin you did not leave us in our sin;
> but you came to us in the person of Jesus Christ,
> who lived among us,
> died for our sin,
> was resurrected,
> ascended into heaven,
> and will return to renew the earth and establish his kingdom forever.
> Bless us as we worship in his name.

I said to myself, "There it is. That's it. There is the story of the world, the truth about human existence." Worship does truth. It tells and enacts God's story—how God rescues creatures and creation. It's in our hymns and choruses, in our Scripture reading and preaching, in our prayers, and supremely in the thanksgiving we make over bread and wine.

Sunday worship, every Sunday, is a celebration of God's story. And the constant bathing of our worship in this story—songs, preaching, baptism, Eucharist, and the Christian-year celebrations—form and shape our conscious and unconscious living in this theater of God's glory!

Sunday Is an Experience of God's Renewing Presence

A second unique aspect of Sunday after Sunday worship is the experience of God's presence. In recent years worshipers have been polled on whether or not they have experienced God's presence in worship. The most common answer is "No." I think this response derives from a fundamental misunderstanding of how God is made present. I think many people are looking for a warm fuzzy and are missing the more obvious ways in which God's presence is manifested in the worship of God's people.

Let me start with a biblical axiom: *The presence of God is always manifested in visible and tangible signs. Our calling in worship is to be open and vulnerable to God's presence so that it becomes embodied in our lives.* The Bible abounds with examples of God's presence communicated in visible signs. A few examples will suffice. Moses experienced the presence of God in the burning bush. By being open, he heard God's call. He embodied this call and marched into Egypt to demand the release of God's people. After God brought the people up out of Egypt, God instructed them to build a tabernacle where "I will dwell among them" (Exod. 25:8). For those who knew how to see, God's presence was evident. They knew that God dwelt there in the tabernacle in the holy of holies over the ark between the cherubim. And this shaped their lives to discern God's presence and live in obedience to his word.

The supreme act of God's presence occurred in the incarnation. The Word was made flesh and tabernacled among us. God was made visible as Jesus in the flesh. In his flesh he lived among us, was crucified on the cross, buried, and resurrected, and then he remained among his disciples teaching them and forming them into his image. But after forty days he ascended into heaven and has never been seen again. Or has he?

Here is the issue. I am sure some of us say, "I wish he was here. I wish I could see him, touch him, walk with him, and hear his voice." We can. It is unthinkable that Jesus would leave us and not provide us with signs of his presence. Fortunately, he has not left us to be alone without tangible and concrete signs of his presence.

He has sent the Holy Spirit who lives within us. The first sign of his presence in Sunday worship is the assembled people. What does this say about our hospitality toward each other? Do we experience the presence of God in the warmth and hospitality of those assembled people? The rule of thumb is this: Our God is a welcoming God, and people experience God's welcome in the welcoming of God's people. This is an experience of God's presence. But God is present in our worship in other ways as well.

God is present in the ministry. We are all ministers by virtue of the priesthood of all believers. But there are among us those who have been ordained to be the chief minister. These persons are to be a special sign of the ministry of Jesus, for Jesus came as servant. He came among us not that we would minister to him but that he might be our minister, the servant among us. All of us are to be ministers after the likeness of Jesus' ministry. And those who are the chief ministers among us are to model the ministry of Jesus who ministers through them. So when one asks, "Did you experience the presence of God in that worship community?" the answer may be, "Oh yes! That minister is such a servant that through his or her ministry Christ was made unusually present to me." God's presence is known in the visible, tangible sign of the minister among us.

Then there is that very special book, the Bible. It is God's book and as such it is the living voice of God in the midst of the assembly. It speaks words of wisdom; it reproves us, guides us, and comforts us. It must be read, preached, and taught. Through the Bible God takes up a visible and tangible presence among us in such a way that when asked, "Did you experience the presence of God in that worship community?" the answer ought to be, "Oh yes, God was so present in the reading and preaching of his Word. It was as though I was sitting at his feet, as though he was personally speaking to me."

God is also made present through the signs of water, of oil, and of bread and wine. The way the rites of baptism, the anointing with oil, or communion are conducted are powerful moments of presence. Those who administer these sacred actions need to do so with the sense that it is Jesus who baptizes, anoints, or blesses the bread and wine. It is Jesus who looks us in the eye and says, "This is my body given for you. This is my blood shed for you." Worshipers ought to be able to say, "I met Jesus today. He was present at the water, at the anointing with oil, and at the bread and wine."

These, among other signs and symbols used by the Holy Spirit in performative ways, signify God's presence among us. Sunday becomes a most special day. In and through the signs we receive God's presence as we open our hearts to him and make our lives vulnerable to the transformation he communicates.

Sunday Anticipates the Consummation of God's Redeeming Work in the New Heavens and Earth

God's story has a happy ending. It is in fact the drama of human existence. It is not only the story of God who creates and of God who becomes involved in creation to rescue it through the life, death, and resurrection of Christ, it is also the story of the end of history and the forever thereafter. Broadly speaking, dramas fall into two categories—tragic or comedic. A tragic drama has no ending. In the sixties and early seventies tragic dramas were very popular because they expressed the nihilism of that time. I remember especially Samuel Beckett's *Waiting for Godot*. The Wheaton College drama department put on that play, and my youngest daughter, who was in elementary school, had a part. At home we would rehearse her part. "Let's go," she would say, but there was never any place to go because Godot never came. In today's postmodern world the sense of no future, no place to go is upon us once again. Movies, plays, and even some books express our anxiety about the present and fear of the future because postmodernity in many ways is an ultramodernism shaped by the nihilistic attitude of nothing in the present and nothingness in the future.

In the midst of this atmosphere, Sunday worship that is true to what the Christian faith is points to the hope of the world—the expectancy that Christ will come to deliver the ultimate blow to all the powers of evil, destroying them forever. He will establish the new heavens and the new earth. He will reign forever over his redeemed creation. His shalom will rest over all he has made. So Sunday after Sunday the happy ending to the great drama of the world is proclaimed and enacted. It is in our hymns, our Scripture readings, our preaching, and our eucharistic celebration when we do this in remembrance of him until he comes again (1 Cor. 11:26).

So Sundays of ordinary time are not so ordinary. They do truth. They do world history. They do the meaning of human existence. In this doing, we are spiritually formed and shaped by the story that is above all stories through the remembrance of God's mighty acts of salvation, the experience of God's presence through signs and symbols, and the anticipation of a good end to history.

Themes of Ordinary Time

We have seen that the themes of extraordinary time are dictated by the special saving event of each season. These themes are fixed, and the lectionary texts that serve the themes are fixed as well.

In ordinary time the theme is simply God's saving event. Worship planners and preachers have much more flexibility to choose various biblical themes within the overarching theme of salvation history. This flexibility is evident, for example, in the various lectionaries for the Christian year. In ordinary time lectionaries suggest preaching continuously through select books of the Bible. Worship and preaching that follow a particular book of the Bible is called *Lectio Continua*. Evangelicals are fond of this approach to preaching. Indeed, a series of sermons on Romans or some other book of the Bible is especially helpful for the building of knowledge and has been followed very successfully in many evangelical churches.

I think a valid way to form congregational spirituality through the Christian year is to follow the lectionary texts from Advent to Pentecost, then do a book of the Bible during ordinary time. The lectionary suggests books to exegete, but I think it is appropriate to follow your interests during this season or speak to the special needs of the congregation with a series of sermons on a particular theme or truth.

There are special days that are celebrated during the Sundays of ordinary time after Pentecost. The first of these days is Trinity Sunday. It falls on the first Sunday after Pentecost, and rightly so. At Pentecost Jesus is declared to be both Messiah and Lord (Acts 2:36 NRSV) and, of course, that is the day for the coming of the Holy Spirit. The Christian church, following the Pentecostal experience, has always been committed to a triune experience and understanding of God, but most preachers seldom preach on this subject. The discipline of addressing the congregation once a year on the meaning of triune faith and worship is helpful and even necessary. I say *necessary* because in today's world of New Age monism and Islamic oneness, Christians need to know not only the *why* of the trinitarian God but also the spiritual understanding of the self made in the image of God and the significance of Christian community that mirrors the eternal, communal relationship of Father, Son, and Holy Spirit.

A second important Sunday in ordinary time is All Saints' Day. It always falls on the weekend after Halloween, which is a secularization of the historic day of All Saints. In today's world many parents are becoming alarmed by the entrance of the occult into the celebration of Halloween. A good antidote to the underworld themes of Halloween is to return to the real meaning of All Saints' Day—a celebration of the life and witness of God's people who model a relationship with God for us. A great hymn that every child should learn by heart is "For All the Saints." Sing this hymn on All Saints' Day and preach on the model life of those whom we remember on that special occasion.

Thanksgiving Day can also be made into a special Sunday celebration. It bears a similarity to the Feast of the Harvest in the Old Testament and can be connected to that festive occasion when God is thanked. On the last Sunday before Advent, the church celebrates the Feast of Christ the King or what is also called the Feast of the Reign of Christ. This is a very important feast day that should not be disregarded. The Feast of

Christ the King is an appropriate segue into Advent, which begins with the eschatological longing for the new heavens and the new earth.

The Feast of Christ the King is of modern origin. It was instituted in 1925 to function in a countercultural way against the secularization of the modern world. It is needed now more than ever as the time before Christmas has become saturated by consumerism, crowding out the real meaning of the season. By pointing to the ultimate reign of Christ over all the peoples of the world, over all nations, and over the entire cosmos, the church prepares its people to approach Christmas in the right spirit—the babe has come to die for our sin, to conquer all the powers of evil, and to reign as Lord over his entire creation! In this expectation we are to be spiritually formed. By bowing our knees to Christ we are inviting the cosmic Lord of history to take up residence in our hearts and lives and to be Lord of life now in this and in every moment of our thoughts, feelings, and actions.[1]

Conclusion

I have attempted to show that ordinary time is not so ordinary. While extraordinary time celebrates a specific saving event in the birth, life, death, and resurrection of Jesus, the Sundays of ordinary time celebrate the saving events of God in their entirety. Worship planners and preachers need to reflect on how each Sunday serves the whole story yet also teaches a particular theme arising from the story. A conscious, deliberate, and intentional reflection on the whole story and a part of the story, celebrated in the same service, impacts the worshipers' spiritual formation.

The whole story keeps us in the Christian vision that sweeps from creation, fall, incarnation, death, resurrection, and second coming. The particular emphasis on a specific doctrine, ethic, mission, or social action keeps our faith focused on an action that embodies truth and witnesses to God's kingdom.

Table 9: A Summary of Spirituality after Pentecost

Theme	Spiritual Emphasis
What is the theme of ordinary time?	The theme of ordinary time is the Sunday by Sunday celebration of the death and resurrection of Jesus Christ.
Why was Sunday called "the eighth day" in the early church?	On the first day of the week (Sunday) God created the heavens and the earth. On the Sabbath (Saturday) God rested. On Sunday Christ rose from the dead to begin again the creation. Thus the seventh day (Saturday) and the day of the resurrection (Sunday) constitute a new beginning for the world (the eighth day).

What does Sunday do?	It remembers God's saving action in history.
	It is an experience of God's renewing presence.
	It anticipates God's redeeming work in the new heavens and the new earth.
What are some of the special Sundays of ordinary time?	Trinity Sunday
	All Saints' Day
	The Feast of Christ the King

A Prayer for Ordinary Time

Remember, O Lord, what you have wrought in us and not what we deserve; and, as you have called us to your service, make us worthy of our calling; through Jesus Christ our Lord, who lives and reigns with you and the Holy Spirit, one God, now and forever. Amen.

From *The Book of Common Prayer*

Questions for Reflection

1. Does your Sunday worship point you to a remembrance of God's mighty acts of salvation?
2. How does the image of the eighth day help you to gain a Christian perspective on world history?
3. How will you live out an after Pentecost spirituality?

Resources for Ordinary Time Worship and Preaching

See Robert Webber, ed., *The Services of the Christian Year*, vol. 5 of *The Complete Library of Christian Worship* (Peabody, MA: Hendrickson, 1994), 427–95.

- Worship on Pentecost Sunday
- Resources for the season after Pentecost
- Resources for other commemorations in the Christian calendar

EPILOGUE

Now that we have come to the end of the book, *Ancient-Future Time*, I must ask, how do you practice time? Is time in your life a constraint or a rhythm?

I am afraid that for many of us, including myself, time is seen as a constraint. I often wish I had more time. If only I had more time that lecture would be better prepared, that manuscript would be complete, that relationship with my spouse, my children, my grandchildren, my neighbors, my fellow workers would be better. For many of us the day has too few hours, the week too few days, the month too few weeks. The year has gone by and the projects we have hoped to finish are not yet completed. Oh the tyranny of time! It moves with such speed that hopes are dashed by its quick demise into yesterday, never to be repeated or recovered.

But there is another approach to time that avoids the tyranny of constraint. In this practice time is not constrictive but freeing. It is experiencing time as rhythm. We find this practice of time taught in the early church and by contemplatives throughout history. I believe it is possible to borrow the practice of time from the ancients and learn to live in the rhythm of freeing time in the midst of our busy world.

Time that is freeing begins with the rhythm of the day. The roots for the rhythm of daily time lie in temple worship in the Jewish tradition (see Acts 3:1). This rhythm was translated into a Christian experience of the day. For example, Hippolytus in *The Apostolic Tradition*, written in the early part of the third century, reports the following daily rhythm of prayer:

9 AM   Meditate on the suffering of Christ for at that hour Christ was nailed to the tree.

Noon   Meditate on the suffering of Christ for at that hour all creation became dark.

3 PM   Meditate on the death of Christ. For at that hour he died.[1]

What if the principle of the early church was translated to form our day into a conscious Christian rhythm of daily devotion? By remembering the work of Christ on the cross at 9 AM, noon, and 3 PM, we would experience each day in the rhythm of the most central event of human history. Add to those hours the remembrance of creation on rising and an anticipation of the new heavens and the new earth at the coming again upon retiring and the rhythm of the day will express the contours of all history.

Next, the rhythmic experience of time moves to Sunday worship. I have already commented on the significance of Sunday as a day to remember God's saving deeds in history and to anticipate God's culmination of history in the new heavens and new earth. While Sunday is still a day of the week, one could do the devotion of the day and add to it a daily devotion that would allow for a brief additional time during the day to reflect on the meaning of Sunday. Sunday is not only the day to remember creation and redemption and to look forward to the new heavens and new earth, but it is also a time to gather in the Christian community to celebrate the meaning of history and of human existence as it is interpreted through Jesus Christ. It is the eighth day, the day when God both rests from his work of creation and the day we celebrate the new beginning God gives the creation as it moves toward its final moment of redemption in the second coming. So Sunday is the day to not only pause to remember but to actually proclaim and enact God's mighty deeds of salvation to the glory of God. For through this day all time and all history is given meaning.

Finally, the rhythm of the Christian year, particularly that of the extraordinary season from Advent to Pentecost, would guide the Christian through a variety of times and emotions. As we have seen:

Advent is a time to *wait*.

Christmas is a time to *rejoice*.

Epiphany is a time to *witness*.

Lent is a time for *repentance and renewal*.

The Great Triduum is a time to *enter death*.

Easter is a time to *express the resurrected life*.

After Pentecost is a time to *study and evangelize*.

Of course we are to do all of these Christian practices all of the time. But a rule of thumb is that a specific time set aside for each facilitates and empowers our Christian experience at all times.

I am persuaded that the practice of Christian time—personally and in the church—will establish a rhythm of time that will free us. It will release us from time as an evil power that tyrannizes our lives to a time that frees us to live in the rhythm of the death and resurrection of Jesus—a pattern that will keep us in an unceasing spirituality.

NOTES

Chapter 1: Ordering Your Spiritual Life

1. James Rowe, "I Would Be Like Jesus," 1912.

2. Adolf Adam, *The Liturgical Year: Its History and Its Meaning after the Reform of the Liturgy* (Collegeville, MN: Liturgical Press, 1992), vii

3. Robert Taft, *Beyond East and West: Problems in Liturgical Understanding* (Washington, DC: Pastoral Press, 1984), 4.

4. Ibid., 32.

5. Adam, *The Liturgical Year: Its History and Meaning*, 40.

6. "The Constitution on the Sacred Liturgy," no. 106, in *Documents of Vatican II*, ed. Austin P. Flannery (Grand Rapids: Eerdmans, 1975), 29–30.

7. Ibid., 29.

8. Adrian Nocent, *The Liturgical Year: Advent, Christmas, Epiphany* (Collegeville, MN: Liturgical Press, 1977), 15.

9. Leo the Great, *Sermo* 37, 1 (CCL 138A:307), quoted in Nocent, *The Liturgical Year: Advent, Christmas, Epiphany*, 17.

Chapter 2: Advent

1. The *Rorate Caeli*, which takes its name from Isaiah 45:8, is essentially a Christian meditation based on Isaiah 64.

2. Irenaeus, *Against Heresies*, Book V, 19, in Cyril Richardson, *Early Christian Fathers* (Philadelphia: Westminster Press, 1953), 389–90.

3. Eucharistic Prayer D, *The Book of Common Prayer* (New York: Seabury Press, 1979), 374.

4. "O Come, O Come, Emmanuel," thirteenth-century Latin hymn, trans. John M. Neale.

Chapter 3: Christmas

1. Leo the Great, *Sermo* 29, 1 (CCL 138:147), quoted in Nocent, *The Liturgical Year: Advent, Christmas, Epiphany*, 190.

2. "O Come, O Come, Emmanuel," thirteenth-century Latin hymn, trans. John M. Neale.

3. Ibid.

4. *The Book of Common Prayer*, 161.

5. Aurelius C. Prudentius, "Of the Father's Love Begotten," fourth-century hymn, trans. John M. Neale (1854) and Henry W. Baker (1859).

6. *The Book of Common Prayer*, 366.

7. Irenaeus, *Against Heresies*, in Richardson, *Early Christian Fathers*.

8. *Book of Divine Prayers and Services of the Catholic Orthodox Church of Christ*, comp. Reverend Seraphim Nassar (Englewood, NJ: Antiochene Orthodox Christian Archdiocese of North America, 1979).

9. Ibid., 393.

10. L. Brou, "Saint Gregoire de Naziance et L'ancienne *mirabile mysterium* des Laudes de la Circoncision," *Ephemerides Liturgicae* 58 (1944), quoted in Nocent, *The Liturgical Year: Advent, Christmas, Epiphany*, 204.

11. *The Sacramentary* (New York: Catholic Book Publishing, 1985), 37.

12. French trans. by Gouillard, *Petite Philocalie* (Paris: Editions des Cahiers du Sud, 1953), 58, quoted in John Meyendorff, *St. Gregory Palamas and Orthodox Spirituality* (Crestwood, NY: St. Vladimir's Seminary Press, 1974), 24.

Chapter 4: Epiphany

1. Charles Coffin, "What Star Is This, With Beams So Bright?" (Chicago: Covenant Press, 1973).

2. *The Book of Common Prayer*, 162.

3. St. Gregory of Nyssa, *The Bible and the Liturgy*, trans. Jean Cardinal Danielou, quoted in Nocent, *The Liturgical Year: Advent, Christmas, Epiphany*, 279.

4. *Book of Divine Prayers and Services*, 467–68.

5. R. M. French, trans., *The Way of the Pilgrim* (New York: Seabury Press, 1965), 8–9.

6. Nicodemus of the Holy Mountain, ed., *Unseen Warfare*, rev. Theophan the Recluse (Crestwood, NY: St. Vladimir's Seminary Press, 2000), 215–18.

Chapter 5: Lent

1. *The Book of Common Prayer*, 264.

2. Ibid., 264–65.

3. Ibid., 265.

4. See "The Litany of Penitence," *The Book of Common Prayer*, 267–69.

5. *The Book of Common Prayer*, 268.

6. Ibid.

7. Ibid.

8. See Alexander Schmemann, *Great Lent* (Crestwood, NY: St. Vladimir's Seminary Press, 1969).

9. *Didache* 7. See Cyril Richardson, *Early Christian Fathers*, 174.

10. See *The Book of Common Prayer*, 302–3.

11. St. Ephrem the Syrian, quoted in Schmemann, *Great Lent*, 34.

12. See the service for Palm Sunday in *The Book of Common Prayer*, 270.

13. Ibid., 271.

14. Theodulph of Orleans, "All Glory, Laud and Honor," trans. John M. Neale.

15. *The Book of Common Prayer*, 272.

16. Ibid., 363.

17. Venatius Fortunatus, "The Royal Banners Forward Go," trans. John M. Neale.

Chapter 6: The Great Triduum

1. St. Ambrose, quoted in Adrian Nocent, *The Liturgical Year: The Easter Season* (Collegeville, MN: Liturgical Press, 1977), 28.

2. *The Book of Common Prayer*, 274.

3. Ibid., 275.

4. For samples of the Maundy Thursday service, see Robert Webber, ed., *The Services of the Christian Year*, vol. 5 of *The Complete Library of Christian Worship* (Peabody, MA: Hendrickson, 1994), 317–34.

5. For a Way of the Cross service, see ibid., 358–63.

6. For Good Friday services, especially the Veneration of the Cross, see ibid., 335–48.

7. For the Great Paschal Vigil, see ibid., 373–96.

Chapter 7: Easter

1. Adolf Harnack, *What Is Christianity?* (reprint, New York: Harper and Row, 1957), 160.

2. Greg Wilde, e-mail correspondence to author, 16 May 2003.

3. Melito of Sardis, quoted in G. F. Hawthorne, ed., *Current Issues in Biblical and Patristic Interpretation* (Grand Rapids: Eerdmans, 1975), 173.

4. St. Leo the Great, quoted in Adrian Nocent, *The Liturgical Year: The Easter Season*, 173–74.

5. David Bunker, lecture delivered at Northern Baptist Seminary, 29 April 2003.

6. For Easter season resources see Robert Webber, *The Complete Library of Christian Worship*, 407–26.

7. Leo the Great, quoted in Nocent, *The Liturgical Year: The Easter Season*, 233.

8. For ascension resources see Robert Webber, *The Complete Library of Christian Worship*, 413–15.

9. For Pentecost resources see ibid., 427–56.

Chapter 8: After Pentecost

1. For resources for ordinary time see Robert Webber, *The Complete Library of Christian Worship*, 457–92.

Epilogue

1. See Burton Scott Easton, *The Apostolic Tradition of Hippolytus* (Hamden: Archon Books, 1962), 20.

BIBLIOGRAPHY

General Resources

Reference Works

Hickman, Hoyt L., Don E. Saliers, Laurence Hull Stookey, and James F. White. *The New Handbook of the Christian Year*. Nashville: Abingdon, 1992.

Webber, Robert, ed. *The Services of the Christian Year*. Vol. 5 of *The Complete Library of Christian Worship*. Peabody, MA: Hendrickson, 1994.

The Church Fathers

Barnecut, Edith, ed. *Journey with the Fathers*. 2 vols. *Commentaries on the Sunday Gospel*. Hyde Park, NY: New City Press, 1993.

Forell, George W. *The Christian Year: Sermons of the Fathers*. 2 vols. New York: Nelson, 1965.

Halton, Thomas, and Thomas Carroll. *Liturgical Practice in the Fathers*. Wilmington, DE: Glazier, 1988.

Introductions and Studies

Adam, Adolf. *The Liturgical Year: Its History and Its Meaning after the Reform of the Liturgy*. Collegeville, MN: Liturgical Press, 1992.

Blackburn, Bonnie, and Leofranc Holford-Stevens. *The Oxford Companion of the Year: An Exploration of Calendar Customs and Time-Reckoning*. Oxford: Oxford University Press, 1999.

Bosch, Paul. *Church Year Guide*. Minneapolis: Augsburg, 1987.

Chilton, Bruce. *Redeeming Time*. Peabody, MA: Hendrickson, 2002.

Hynes, Mary Ellen, et al. *Companion to the Calendar: A Guide to the Saints and Mysteries of the Christian Calendar*. Chicago: Liturgy Training Publications, 1993.

Liturgical Year: The Worship of God. Supplemental Liturgical Resource 7. Louisville: Westminster/John Knox, 1992.

Martimort, A. G., Irenee Henri Dalmais, and Pierre Jounel. *The Church at Prayer: The Liturgy and Time*. London: Geoffrey Chapman, 1983.

Metford, J. C. J. *The Christian Year*. London: Thomas and Hudson, 1991.

Monk of the Eastern Church. *The Year of Grace of the Lord: A Scriptural and Liturgical Commentary on the Calendar of the Orthodox Church*. Crestwood, NY: St. Vladimir's Seminary Press, 1980.

Talley, Thomas J. *The Origins of the Liturgical Year*. New York: Pueblo Publishing, 1986.

Whalen, Michael D. *Seasons and Feasts of the Church Year: An Introduction*. New York: Paulist, 1993.

White, James F. *Introduction to Christian Worship*. Rev. ed. Nashville: Abingdon, 1990. Chapters 2 and 4.

Christian-Year Spirituality

Belisle, Augustine. *The Wheel of Becoming*. Petersham, MA: St. Bede's Publications, 1987.

Cowie, L. W., and John Selwyn Gummer. *The Christian Calendar: A Complete Guide to the Seasons of the Christian Year Telling the Story of Christ and the Saints from Advent to Pentecost*. Springfield, MA: G & C Merriam Company, 1974.

Every, George, Richard Harries, and Kallistos Ware, eds. *The Time of the Spirit: Readings through the Christian Year*. Crestwood, NY: St. Vladimir's Seminary Press, 1984.

Halmo, Joan. *Celebrating the Church Year with Young Children*. Collegeville, MN: Liturgical Press, 1988.

Hammerton, Kelly, and Robert Hammerton. *Spring Time: Seasons of the Christian Year*. Nashville: Upper Room, 1980.

Johnson, Lawrence, ed. *The Church Gives Thanks and Remembers: Essays on the Liturgical Year*. Collegeville, MN: Liturgical Press, 1984.

Johnson, Maxwell E. *Between Memory and Hope: Readings on the Liturgical Year*. Collegeville, MN: Liturgical Press, 2000.

Kay, James E. *Seasons of Grace: Reflections from the Christian Year*. Grand Rapids: Eerdmans, 1994.

L'Engle, Madeleine. *The Irrational Season*. New York: Crosswicks, 1977.

The Liturgical Year: Celebrating the Mystery of Christ and His Saints. Washington, DC: Bishops Committee on the Liturgy, United States Catholic Conference, 1985.

Nardone, Richard M. *The Story of the Christian Year*. New York: Paulist, 1991.

Nocent, Adrian. *The Liturgical Year*. 4 vols. Collegeville, MN: Liturgical Press, 1977.

O'Driscoll, Herbert. *A Year of the Lord: Reflections of the Christian Faith from the Advent of the Christ Child to the Reign of Christ as King*. Wilton, CT: Morehouse-Barlow, 1986.

Peterson, Eugene, and Emilie Griffin, eds. *Epiphanies: Stories for the Christian Year*. Grand Rapids: Baker, 2003.

Porter, Boone H. *Keeping the Church Year*. New York: Seabury, 1977.

Power, David, ed. *The Times of Celebration*. Concillium No. 142. New York: Seabury, 1981.

Preston, Geoffrey. *Hallowing the Time*. New York: Paulist, 1980.

Stookey, Laurence Hull. *Calendar: Christ's Time for the Church*. Nashville: Abingdon, 1996.

Toulson, Shirley. *The Celtic Year: A Celebration of Celtic Christian Saints, Sites and Festivals.* Rockport, MA: Element, 1993.

Westerhoff, John H., III. *A Pilgrim People: Learning through the Church Year.* New York: Seabury, 1984.

Wilde, James A., ed. *At That Time: Cycles and Seasons of the Christian Year.* Chicago: Liturgy Training Publications, 1989.

General Resources for Planning and Leading Christian-Year Worship

Planning Resources

Hartgen, William E. *Planning Guide for Lent and Holy Week.* Glendale, AZ: Pastoral Arts Associates, 1979.

Mitchell, Lionel L. *Planning the Church Year.* Harrisburg, PA: Morehouse Publishing, 1991.

Prayer Book Resources

Book of Common Prayer. New York: Church Hymnal Corp., 1979.

Book of Common Worship. Louisville: Westminster/John Knox, 1992.

Book of Divine Prayers and Services of the Catholic Orthodox Church of Christ. Compiled and arranged by the late Reverend Seraphim Nassar. Englewood, NJ: Antiochene Orthodox Christian Archdiocese of North America, 1979.

Book of Occasional Services: The Proper for Lesser Feasts and Fasts. New York: Church Hymnal Corp., 1990.

Book of Worship: United Church of Christ. New York: United Church of Christ, 1986.

Lutheran Book of Worship. Minneapolis: Augsburg, and Philadelphia: Board of Publication, Lutheran Church in America, 1978.

Pfatteicher, Philip H. *Festivals and Commemorations.* Minneapolis: Augsburg, 1980.

Pray to the Lord. New York: Reformed Church Press, 1988.

The Roman Missal: Lectionary for Mass. New York: Catholic Book Publishing, 1970.

The Roman Missal: The Sacramentary. New York: Catholic Book Publishing, 1974.

Seasons of the Gospel: Resources for the Christian Year. Nashville: Abingdon, 1979.

The United Methodist Book of Worship. Nashville: United Methodist Publishing House, 1992.

Worship Resources. Worship Series No. 12. Newton, KS: Mennonite Publishing House, 1978.

Lectionary Sources

Borsch, Frederick Houk. *Introducing the Lessons of the Church Year: A Guide for Lay Leaders and Congregations.* New York: Seabury, 1978.

Companion to the Lectionary. 4 vols. London: Epworth Press, 1987.

Every, George, Richard Harries, and Kallistos Ware, eds. *The Time of the Spirit: Readings through the Christian Year*. Crestwood, NY: St. Vladimir's Seminary Press, 1984.

Jarrell, Stephen T. *Guide to the Sacramentary*. Chicago: Liturgy Training Publications, 1983.

Lathrop, Gordon, and Gail Ramshaw Schmidt. *Lectionary for the Christian People*. 3 vols. Cycle A, B, C. New York: Pueblo Publishing, 1986, 1987, 1988.

Mills, Douglas W. *A Daily Lectionary: Scripture Readings for Every Day Based on the New Common Lectionary*. Nashville: Upper Room, 1986.

Ramshaw, Gail. *Richer Fare: Reflections on the Sunday Readings of Cycles A, B, C*. New York: Pueblo Publishing, 1990.

Wood, Geoff. *Living the Lectionary: Links to Life and Literature*. Year C. Chicago: Liturgy Training Publications, 2003.

Preaching Resources

Achtemeier, Elizabeth Rice. *Preaching and Reading the Old Testament Lessons: With an Eye to the New*. 3 vols. Cycle A, B, C. Lima, OH: CSS Publishing, 1991–1993.

Alling, Roger, and David J. Schlafer. *Preaching through Holy Days and Holidays*. Harrisburg, PA: Morehouse, 2003.

Bergant, Dianne, and Richard Fragomeni. *Preaching the New Lectionary*. 2 vols. Cycle A and B. Collegeville, MN: Liturgical Press, Year B 1999, Year A 2001.

Burger, L. W., B. A. Miller, and D. J. Smit. *Sermon Guides for Preaching in Easter, Ascension, and Pentecost*. Grand Rapids: Eerdmans, 1988.

Craddock, Fred B., John H. Hayes, Carl R. Holladay, and Gene M. Tucker. *Preaching through the Christian Year*. 3 vols. Philadelphia: Trinity Press International, 1992.

Days of the Lord: The Liturgical Year. 7 vols. Collegeville, MN: Liturgical Press, 1991–1994.

Dozeman, Thomas, Kendall McCabe, and Marion Soards. *Preaching the Revised Common Lectionary*. 12 vols. Nashville: Abingdon, 1992–93.

Duckworth, Robin. *This Is the Word of the Lord*. 3 vols. London: Bible Reading Fellowship and New York: Oxford University Press, 1982.

Fuller, Reginald. *Preaching the Lectionary: The Word of God for the Church Today*. Collegeville, MN: Liturgical Press, 1984.

Hessel, Dieter T. *Social Themes of the Christian Year*. Philadelphia: Geneva Press, 1983.

Lowry, Eugene. *Living with the Lectionary*. Nashville: Abingdon, 1992.

Maestri, William F. *Grace Upon Grace: Biblical Homilies for Sunday and Holy Days*. Cycles A, B, and C. New York: Alba House, 1988.

Maly, Eugene H. *The Word Alive: Commentaries and Reflections on the Scripture Readings for all Sundays, Solemnities of the Lord, Holy Days, and Major Feasts of the Three Year Cycle*. New York: Alba House, 1982.

Ramshaw, Gail, ed. *Homiletics for Christian People*. Cycle A, B, C. New York: Pueblo Publishing, 1989.

The Revised Common Lectionary. Consultation on Common Texts. Nashville: Abingdon, 1992.

Walker, Michael. *From Glory to Glory: Biblical Reflections from Advent to the Feast of Christ the King*. London: Collins Liturgical Press, 1978.

Readings and Prayers

Cones, Bryan M. *Daily Prayer: A Book of Prayer, Psalms, Sacred Readings and Reflections in Tune with the Seasons, Feasts, and Ordinary Days of the Year*. Chicago: Liturgy Training Publications, published yearly.

Crouch, Timothy J., Nancy B. Crouch, Chris Vismanis, and Mark R. Babb. *And Also with You*. 3 vols. Cleveland: OSL Publications, 1992–1994.

Daily Prayer: The Worship of God. Prepared by the office of worship for the Presbyterian Church (U.S.A.) and the Cumberland Presbyterian Church. Philadelphia: Westminster Press, 1987.

Deiss, Lucien. *Come Lord Jesus: Biblical Prayers with Psalms and Scripture Readings*. Chicago: World Library Publications, 1981.

Duck, Ruth C. *Bread for the Journey: Resources for Worship*. New York: Pilgrim Press, 1981.

———. *Flames of the Spirit*. New York: Pilgrim Press, 1987.

———. *Touch Holiness*. New York: Pilgrim Press, 1990.

Hostettler, B. David. *Psalms and Prayers for Congregational Participation*. 3 vols. Lima, OH: CSS Publishing, 1985.

Karay, Diane. *All the Seasons of Mercy*. Philadelphia: Westminster, 1987.

Kirk, James G. *When We Gather: A Book of Prayers for Worship*. 3 vols. Philadelphia: Geneva Press, 1985.

Konstant, David. *Bidding Prayers for the Church's Year*. Great Wakering, Essex, U.K.: Mayhew-McCrimmon Press, 1976, 1982.

O'Donnell, Michael. *Lift Up Your Hearts*. 3 vols. Cleveland: OSL Publications, 1989–1991.

Perham, Michael. *Enriching the Christian Year*. Collegeville, MN: Liturgical Press, 1993.

Pfatteicher, Philip H. *Festivals and Commemorations*. Minneapolis: Augsburg, 1980.

The Proper for the Lesser Feasts and Fasts Together with the Fixed Holy Days. 4th ed. New York: Church Hymnal Corp., 1988.

Shepherd, Massey H. *A Liturgical Psalter for the Christian Year*. Minneapolis: Augsburg, 1976.

Tilson, Everett, and Phyllis Cole. *Liturgies and Other Prayers for the Revised Common Lectionary*. 3 vols. Nashville: Abingdon, 1992–1994.

Webber, Robert. *The Book of Family Prayer*. Peabody, MA: Hendrickson, 1986.

Music and the Arts

Bone, David L., and Mary J. Scifres. *The United Methodist Music and Worship Planner*. Nashville: Abingdon, 1992.

Christian Worship: A Lutheran Hymnal. Milwaukee: Northwestern Publishing House, 1993.

Erspamer, Steve. *Clip Art for Year A*. Chicago: Liturgy Training Publications, 1992.

The Hymnal, 1982: According to the Use of the Episcopal Church. New York: Church Hymnal Corp., 1985.

Lonneman, Julie. *Clip Art for Sundays and Solemnities*. Chicago: Liturgy Training Publications, 2003.

Psalter Hymnal. Grand Rapids: CRC Publications, 1987.

Schmidt, Clemens. *Clip Art for the Christian Year*. Collegeville, MN: Liturgical Press, 1988.

Troeger, Thomas, and Carol Doran. *New Hymns for the Lectionary to Glorify the Maker's Name*. New York: Oxford University Press, 1986.

Wetzler, Robert, and Helen Huntington. *Seasons and Symbols: A Handbook on the Church Year*. Minneapolis: Augsburg, 1962.

The Worshiping Church: A Hymnal. Carol Stream, IL: Hope Publishing, 1990.

Specific Resources for the Cycles of Light and Life

Resources for the Cycle of Light: Advent, Christmas, Epiphany

Brokhoff, John R. *Advent and Event*. Lima, OH: CSS Publishing, 1980.

Brown, Raymond E. *An Adult Christ for Christmas*. Collegeville, MN: Liturgical Press, 1977.

———. *A Coming Christ in Advent*. Collegeville, MN: Liturgical Press, 1988.

Buckland, Patricia. *Advent to Pentecost*. Wilton, CT: Morehouse-Barlow, 1979.

Griffin, Eltin, ed. *Celebrating the Season of Advent*. Collegeville, MN: Liturgical Press, 1986.

Groh, Dennis E. *In Between Advents*. Philadelphia: Fortress, 1986.

Hopko, Thomas. *The Winter Pascha: Readings for the Christmas-Epiphany Season*. Crestwood, NY: St. Vladimir's Seminary Press, 1984.

Irwin, Kevin W. *Advent-Christmas: A Guide to the Eucharist and the Hours*. New York: Pueblo Publishing, 1986.

Kirk, James G. *Meditations for Advent and Christmas*. Louisville: Westminster/John Knox, 1989.

Payne, Donna W., and Fran Zeno. *The Handel's Messiah Family Advent Reader*. Chicago: Moody Press, 1999.

Perham, Michael, and Kenneth Stevenson. *Welcoming the Light of Christ*. Collegeville, MN: Liturgical Press, 1991.

The Promise of His Glory: Services and Prayers for the Season from All Saints to Candlemas. Collegeville, MN: Liturgical Press, 1991.

Rest, Friedrich. *Our Christian Worship*. Lima, OH: CSS Publishing, 1985.

Simcoe, Mary Ann, ed. *A Christmas Source Book*. Chicago: Liturgy Training Publications, 1984.

Resources for the Cycle of Life: Lent, Holy Week, the Great Triduum, Easter

Aho, Gerhard, Kenneth Rogahn, and Richard Hapfer. *Glory in the Cross: Fruit of the Spirit from the Passion of Christ*. St. Louis: Concordia Press, 1984.

Akehurst, Peter R. *Keeping Holy Week*. Brancote, Notts, U.K.: Grove Books, 1976.

Bibliography

Berger, Rupert, and Hans Hollerweger, eds. *Celebrating the Easter Vigil*. Translated by Matthew J. O'Connell. New York: Pueblo Publishing, 1983.

Boyer, Mark G. *Mystagogy*. New York: Alba House, 1990.

Chilson, Richard. *A Lenten Pilgrimage*. New York: Paulist, 1981.

Cotter, Theresa. *What Color Is Your Lent?* Cincinnati: St. Anthony Messenger Press, 1987.

Crichton, J. D. *The Liturgy of Holy Week*. Leominster, Herefordshire, U.K.: Fowler Wright Books, 1983.

Flood, Edmund. *Making More of Holy Week*. New York: Paulist, 1983.

Freeman, Eileen Elizabeth. *The Holy Week Book*. San Jose: Resource Publications, 1979.

Greenacre, Roger, and Jeremy Haselock. *The Sacrament of Easter*. Leominster, Herefordshire, U.K.: Gracewing Publications, 1989.

Hopko, Thomas. *The Lenten Spring*. Crestwood, NY: St. Vladimir's Seminary Press, 1983.

Huck, Gabe. *The Three Great Days*. Chicago: Liturgy Training Publications, 1981.

Huck, Gabe, Gail Ramshaw, and Gordon Lathrop, eds. *An Easter Source Book: The Fifty Days*. Chicago: Liturgy Training Publications, 1988.

Huck, Gabe, and Mary Ann Simcoe. *A Triduum Source Book*. Chicago: Liturgy Training Publications, 1983.

MacGregor, A. J. *Fire and Light in the Western Triduum: Their Use at Tenebrae and at Paschal Vigil*. Collegeville, MN: Liturgical Press, 1992.

Manning, Michael. *Pardon My Lenten Smile*. New York: Alba House, 1976.

Nouwen, Henri. *Walk with Jesus: Stations of the Cross*. Maryknoll, NY: Orbis Books, 1990.

Schmemann, Alexander. *Great Lent: Journey to Pascha*. Crestwood, NY: St. Vladimir's Seminary Press, 1974.

Stevenson, Kenneth. *Jerusalem Revisited: The Liturgical Meaning of Holy Week*. Washington, DC: Pastoral Press, 1984.

Thompson, William. *Hands of Lent*. Lima, OH: CSS Publishing, 1989.

Wangerin, Walter. *Reliving the Passion*. St. Louis: Creative Communication for the Parish, 1988.

SUBJECT INDEX

SCRIPTURE INDEX

13:21–35 120
13:31–35 155
13:34 127
14:8–9 156
14:17 156
17 157
17:22 157
17:1 83
18:1–19:42 133
20:1 19, 169

Acts
1:1–11 158
1:3 142, 154, 161
1:8–9 160
2:1–47 142
2:5 162
2:17 20, 162
2:17–21 162
2:36 161, 175
2:37–38 162
2:42–47 150
3:1 179
6:13 69
7 69
7:58 69
10:1–11:18 78

Romans
5:12–21 21, 106
5:18 145
6:1–11 160
6:3–11 21
6:4 21, 146
6:5 146
6:6–7 146
6:8–9 11, 146–47
8:13 113
8:20 145
8:21 28, 89, 145
8:22 145
8:27 162
9:25–26 25
12:1–2 29

1 Corinthians
5:7 25, 82
11:23–26 127

11:20 30
11:23 129
11:26 174
15:12–14 142
15:20–28 106
15:22 28

2 Corinthians
1:5 21
4:5–6 59
4:14 21
5:17 28, 49, 66, 146
5:18 24
5:19 28
5:20–6:10 101

Galatians
2:19–20 21
2:20 21
3:27 21
5:16 66
5:16–24 66
5:19–21 25
5:22–23 25, 66
5:24 25

Ephesians
1:13–14 156
1:18 159
1:21–23 159–60
2:2 113
2:4–10 20
2:5–6 21
2:6 113
3:1–12 78
3:8–10 79
3:10 150, 160

Philippians
1:21 20, 24
2:3 70
2:4 68
2:5–11 68
3:10 21
4:2 67

Colossians
1:17–20 23
1:19 90

Robert E. Webber is the William R. and Geraldyne B. Myers Professor of Ministry at Northern Seminary in Lombard, Illinois, directing the Masters in Worship and Spirituality program. He is the president of the Institute for Worship Studies in Orange Park, Florida, and emeritus professor of theology, Wheaton College.

Webber is the author and editor of more than forty books on worship, including *Worship Old and New*, *Worship Is a Verb*, and *Planning Blended Worship*. He is also the author of *The Younger Evangelicals* and the editor of the *Complete Library of Christian Worship* (eight volumes).

In addition to extensive travel, Webber maintains a strong connection with his readers through his monthly e-newsletter, "Ancient-Future Talk." To subscribe, log on to www.ancientfutureworship.com. Through the message board connected to his website you can converse with others and debate his materials.

ALSO BY ROBERT E. WEBBER

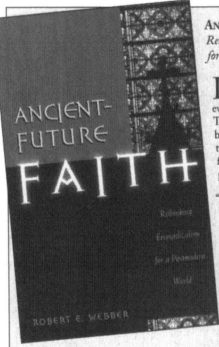

ANCIENT-FUTURE FAITH
*Rethinking Evangelicalism
for a Postmodern World*

IN THIS PROVOCATIVE WORK, Robert E. Webber contends that present-day evangelicalism is a product of modernity. The way forward for evangelicalism begins with looking at the resources the early church tradition provides for making faith relevant in a postmodern world.

"This book makes an important contribution ... as a call for theological renewal within evangelical churches ... timely, practical, and persuasive."

—*Publishers Weekly*

"[A] well written and readable scholarly work with some interesting insights into this important segment of religion in America."

—*Library Journal*

"*The Agenda for Theology,* which I attempted to set forth in 1979, is here being significantly extended by Robert Webber ... in a way that is profoundly gratifying."

— **Thomas C. Oden,** professor of theology and ethics, Drew University

"Here is a faith for our time that finds in the ancient traditions the power to speak to the postmodern world. This book amounts to an introduction to Christianity from the theme of *Christus Victor.* It draws from Webber's own experience of growth as a hearer of God's Word and is backed up with an impressive set of endnotes, charts, and a bibliography."

— **Clark H. Pinnock,** emeritus, McMaster Divinity College

"Robert Webber substantiates the vision of an anciently rooted and forward-looking evangelicalism that marks all of his work. *Ancient-Future Faith* works as a narrative-oriented Christian primer and as a road map to the promise of catholic evangelicalism. ... Webber shows what it means to take seriously the character of Christian testimony as Christ-following church-formed story."

— **Gary Dorrien,** author, *The Remaking of Evangelical Theology*

"Now, more than ever, with the culture wars of a dying modernity cutting deeper and more darkly into desperation and anger, all evangelicalism needs to hear Bob Webber. Take up, read, pray, and consider: in this direction lies the most hopeful future of our faith."

— **Rodney Clapp,** author, *A Peculiar People*

The Younger Evangelicals
Facing the Challenges of the New World

A NEW EVANGELICAL AWAKENING is taking place around the world. And the changes are being introduced by an emerging generation of leaders— *The Younger Evangelicals.* Who are they and what is different about their way of thinking and practicing church? How are they keeping ministry up to speed with our rapidly changing culture? In this provocative and energizing book, they will tell you.

"If you're suspicious about new winds blowing across the evangelical coastland, please don't criticize until you've read The Younger Evangelicals. It is by far the most thoughtful description of what's going on. If you're not critical but just curious, Webber will give you a thorough immersion into the emerging church. And if you're 'younger' yourself or young at heart, you'll find Webber giving voice to much that you have felt but couldn't yet articulate. Webber proves himself a sagely resource for this fresh, fledgling movement in this wise, warm, timely book."

—**Brian McLaren**, pastor, author, senior fellow with Emergent
(www.emergentvillage.com)

"At a time when many graying prognosticators are bemoaning the state of the church, it is refreshing to read a commentator of Robert Webber's stature who is optimistic about the future of the evangelical cause. Webber documents the presence of a cadre whom the Holy Spirit is raising up to lead the church in offering a biblically rooted, historically informed, and culturally aware gospel witness. I am personally encouraged by Webber's findings."

Stanley J. Grenz, Carey Theological College

"An eye-popping, brain-bending look at where the evangelical church must head if it has any hopes of impacting postmodern culture. A superbly researched, foundational work, it is easily the best primer on the emerging church that I have seen."

—**Sally Morgenthaler**, founder of Sacramentis.com, author of *Worship Evangelism*

Meet a NEW GROUP of LEADERS who are SHAPING the FUTURE of a movement

the YOUNGER Evangelicals

Facing the CHALLENGES of the New WORLD

robert e. WEBBER

Made in the USA
Lexington, KY
07 November 2017